Christopher Columbus

and the Discovery of the Americas

Explorers of New Lands

Christopher Columbus
and the Discovery of the Americas

Tim McNeese

Series Consulting Editor William H. Goetzmann
Jack S. Blanton, Sr. Chair in History and American Studies
University of Texas, Austin

CHELSEA HOUSE
PUBLISHERS
A Haights Cross Communications Company ®
Philadelphia

COVER: A portrait of Christopher Columbus

CHELSEA HOUSE PUBLISHERS
VP, NEW PRODUCT DEVELOPMENT Sally Cheney
DIRECTOR OF PRODUCTION Kim Shinners
CREATIVE MANAGER Takeshi Takahashi
MANUFACTURING MANAGER Diann Grasse

Staff for CHRISTOPHER COLUMBUS
EXECUTIVE EDITOR Lee Marcott
EDITORIAL ASSISTANT Carla Greenberg
PRODUCTION EDITOR Noelle Nardone
PHOTO EDITOR Sarah Bloom
COVER AND INTERIOR DESIGNER Keith Trego
LAYOUT 21st Century Publishing and Communications, Inc.

A Haights Cross Communications ✦ Company ®

www.chelseahouse.com

First Printing

9 8 7 6 5 4 3 2 1

Library of Congress Cataloging-in-Publication Data

McNeese, Tim.
    Christopher Columbus: and the discovery of the Americas / Tim McNeese.
        p. cm.—(Explorers of new lands)
    Includes bibliographical references and index.
    ISBN 0-7910-8613-5 (hard cover)
    1. Columbus, Christopher—Juvenile literature. 2. Explorers–America–Biography–Juvenile
literature. 3. Explorers–Spain–Biography–Juvenile literature. 4. America–Discovery and
exploration–Spanish–Juvenile literature. I. Title. II. series.
    E111.M47 2005
    970.01'5'092—dc22

                                                                    2005010071

Table of Contents

Introduction

by William H. Goetzmann
Jack S. Blanton, Sr. Chair in History and American Studies
University of Texas, Austin

Explorers have always been adventurers. They were, and still are, people of vision and most of all, people of curiosity. The English poet Rudyard Kipling once described the psychology behind the explorer's curiosity:

"Something hidden. Go and find it. Go and
   look behind the Ranges—
Something lost behind the Ranges. Lost and
   waiting for you. Go!" [1]

Miguel de Cervantes, the heroic author of *Don Quixote*, longed to be an explorer-conquistador. So he wrote a personal letter to King Phillip II of Spain asking to be appointed to lead an expedition to the New World. Phillip II turned down his request. Later, while in prison, Cervantes gained revenge. He wrote the immortal story of *Don Quixote*, a broken-down, half-crazy "Knight of La Mancha" who "explored" Spain with his faithful sidekick, Sancho Panza. His was perhaps the first of a long line of revenge novels—a lampoon of the real explorer-conquistadors.

Most of these explorer-conquistadors, such as Columbus and Cortés, are often regarded as heroes who discovered new worlds and empires. They were courageous, brave and clever, but most of them were also cruel to the native peoples they met. For example, Cortés, with a small band of 500 Spanish conquistadors, wiped out the vast

Aztec Empire. He insulted the Aztecs' gods and tore down their temples. A bit later, far down in South America, Francisco Pizarro and Hernando de Soto did the same to the Inca Empire, which was hidden behind a vast upland desert among Peru's towering mountains. Both tasks seem to be impossible, but these conquistadors not only overcame nature and savage armies, they stole their gold and became rich nobles. More astounding, they converted whole countries and even a continent to Spanish Catholicism. Cathedrals replaced blood-soaked temples, and the people of South and Central America, north to the Mexican border, soon spoke only two languages—Portuguese in Brazil and Spanish in the rest of the countries, even extending through the Southwest United States.

Most of the cathedral building and language changing has been attributed to the vast numbers of Spanish and Portuguese missionaries, but trade with and even enslavement of the natives must have played a great part. Also playing an important part were great missions that were half churches and half farming and ranching communities. They offered protection from enemies and a life of stability for the natives. Clearly vast numbers of natives took to these missions. The missions vied with the cruel native caciques, or rulers, for protection and for a constant food supply. We have to ask ourselves: Did the Spanish conquests raise the natives' standard of living? And did a religion of love appeal more to the natives than ones of sheer terror, where hearts were torn out and bodies were tossed down steep temple stairways as sacrifices that were probably eaten by dogs or other wild beasts? These questions are something to think about as you read the Explorers of New Lands series. They are profound questions even today.

"New Lands" does not only refer to the Western Hemisphere and the Spanish/Portuguese conquests there. Our series should probably begin with the fierce Vikings—Eric the Red, who discovered Greenland in 982, and Leif Ericson, who discovered North America in 1002, followed, probably a year later, by a settler named Bjorni. The Viking sagas (or tales passed down through generations) tell the stories of these men and of Fredis, the first woman discoverer of a New Land. She became a savior of the Viking men when, wielding a broadsword and screaming like a madwoman, she single-handedly routed the native Beothuks who were about to wipe out the earliest Viking settlement in North America that can be identified. The Vikings did not, however, last as long in North America as they did in Greenland and Northern England. The natives of the north were far tougher than the natives of the south and the Caribbean.

Far away, on virtually the other side of the world, traders were making their way east toward China. Persians and Arabs as well as Mongols established a trade route to the Far East via such fabled cities as Samarkand, Bukhara, and Kashgar and across the Hindu Kush and Pamir Mountains to Tibet and beyond. One of our volumes tells the story of Marco Polo, who crossed from Byzantium (later Constantinople) overland along the Silk Road to China and the court of Kublai Khan, the Mongol emperor. This was a crossing over wild deserts and towering mountains, as long as Columbus's Atlantic crossing to the Caribbean. His journey came under less dangerous (no pirates yet) and more comfortable conditions than that of the Polos, Nicolo and Maffeo, who from 1260 to 1269 made their way across these endless wastes while making friends, not enemies, of the fierce Mongols. In 1271, they took along Marco Polo (who was Nicolo's son and Maffeo's nephew). Marco became a great favorite of Kublai Khan and stayed in China till 1292. He even became the ruler of one of Kublai Khan's largest cities, Hangchow.

Before he returned, Marco Polo had learned of many of the Chinese ports, and because of Chinese trade to the west across the Indian Ocean, he knew of East Africa as far as Zanzibar. He also knew of the Spice Islands and Japan. When he returned to his home city of Venice he brought enviable new knowledge with him, about gunpowder, paper and paper money, coal, tea making, and the role of worms that create silk! While captured by Genoese forces, he dictated an account of his amazing adventures, which included vast amounts of new information, not only about China, but about the geography of nearly half of the globe. This is one hallmark of great explorers. How much did they contribute to the world's body of knowledge? These earlier inquisitive explorers were important members of a culture of science that stemmed from world trade and genuine curiosity. For the Polos, crossing over deserts, mountains and very dangerous tribal-dominated countries or regions, theirs was a hard-won knowledge. As you read about Marco Polo's travels, try and count the many new things and descriptions he brought to Mediterranean countries.

Besides the Polos, however, there were many Islamic traders who traveled to China, like Ibn Battuta, who came from Morocco in Northwest Africa. An Italian Jewish rabbi-trader, Jacob d'Ancona, made his way via India in 1270 to the great Chinese trading port of Zaitun, where he spent much of his time. Both of these explorer-travelers left extensive reports of their expeditions, which rivaled those of the Polos but were less known, as are the neglected accounts of Roman Catholic friars who entered China, one of whom became bishop of Zaitun.[2]

In 1453, the Turkish Empire cut off the Silk Road to Asia. But Turkey was thwarted when, in 1497 and 1498, the Portuguese captain Vasco da Gama sailed from Lisbon around the tip of Africa, up to Arab-controlled Mozambique, and across the

Indian Ocean to Calicut on the western coast of India. He faced the hostility of Arab traders who virtually dominated Calicut. He took care of this problem on a second voyage in 1502 with 20 ships to safeguard the interests of colonists brought to India by another Portuguese captain, Pedro Álvares Cabral. Da Gama laid siege to Calicut and destroyed a fleet of 29 warships. He secured Calicut for the Portuguese settlers and opened a spice route to the islands of the Indies that made Portugal and Spain rich. Spices were valued nearly ✱ as much as gold since without refrigeration, foods would spoil. The spices disguised this, and also made the food taste good. Virtually every culture in the world has some kind of stew. Almost all of them depend on spices. Can you name some spices that come from the faraway Spice Islands?

Of course most Americans have heard of Christopher Columbus, who in 1492 sailed west across the Atlantic for the Indies and China. Instead, on four voyages, he reached Hispaniola (now Haiti and the Dominican Republic), Cuba and Jamaica. He created a vision of a New World, populated by what he misleadingly called Indians.

✱ Columbus mistakenly thought he'd discovered the Indies

+ contradicts idea that Amerigo 1st discovered New World

Conquistadors like the Italian sailing for Portugal, Amerigo Vespucci, followed Columbus and in 1502 reached South America at what is now Brazil. His landing there explains Brazil's Portuguese language origins as well as how America got its name on Renaissance charts drawn on vellum or dried sheepskin.

Meanwhile, the English heard of a Portuguese discovery of marvelous fishing grounds off Labrador (discovered by the Vikings and rediscovered by a mysterious freelance Portuguese sailor named the "Labrador"). They sent John Cabot in 1497 to locate these fishing grounds. He found them, and Newfoundland and Labrador as well. It marked the British discovery of North America.

In this first series there are strange tales of other explorers of new lands—Juan Ponce de León, who sought riches and possibly a fountain of youth (everlasting life) and died in Florida; Francisco Coronado, whose men discovered the Grand Canyon and at Zuñi established what became the heart of the Spanish Southwest before the creation of Santa Fe; and de Soto, who after helping to conquer the Incas, boldly ravaged what is now the

American South and Southeast. He also found that the Indian Mound Builder cultures, centered in Cahokia across the Mississippi from present-day St. Louis, had no gold and did not welcome him. Garcilaso de la Vega, the last Inca, lived to write de Soto's story, called *The Florida of the Inca*—a revenge story to match that of Cervantes, who like Garcilaso de la Vega ended up in the tiny Spanish town of Burgos. The two writers never met. Why was this—especially since Cervantes was the tax collector? Perhaps this was when he was in prison writing *Don Quixote*.

In 1513 Vasco Núñez de Balboa discovered the Pacific Ocean "from a peak in Darien"[3] and was soon beheaded by a rival conquistador. But perhaps the greatest Pacific feat was Ferdinand Magellan's voyage around the world from 1519 to 1522, which he did not survive.

Magellan was a Portuguese who sailed for Spain down the Atlantic and through the Strait of Magellan—a narrow passage to the Pacific. He journeyed across that ocean to the Philippines, where he was killed in a fight with the natives. As a recent biography put it, he had "sailed over the edge of the world."[4] His men continued west, and the *Victoria,* the last of his five ships, worn and battered, reached Spain.

Sir Francis Drake, a privateer and lifelong enemy of Spain, sailed for Queen Elizabeth of England on a secret mission in 1577 to find a passage across the Americas for England. Though he sailed, as he put it, "along the backside of Nueva Espanola"[5] as far north as Alaska perhaps, he found no such passage. He then sailed west around the world to England. He survived to help defeat the huge Spanish Armada sent by Phillip II to take England in 1588. Alas he could not give up his bad habit of privateering, and died of dysentery off Porto Bello, Panama. Drake did not find what he was looking for "beyond the ranges," but it wasn't his curiosity that killed him. He may have been the greatest explorer of them all!

While reading our series of great explorers, think about the many questions that arise in your reading, which I hope inspires you to great deeds.

Notes

1. Rudyard Kipling, "The Explorer" (1898). See Jon Heurtl, *Rudyard Kipling: Selected Poems* (New York: Barnes & Noble Books, 2004), 7.

2. Jacob D'Ancona, David Shelbourne, translator, *The City of Light: The Hidden Journal of the Man Who Entered China Four Years Before Marco Polo* (New York: Citadel Press, 1997).

3. John Keats, "On First Looking Into Chapman's Homer."

4. Laurence Bergreen, *Over the Edge of the World: Magellan's Terrifying Circumnavigation of the Globe* (New York: William Morrow & Company, 2003).

5. See Richard Hakluyt, *Principal Navigations, Voyages, Traffiques and Discoveries of the English Nation*; section on Sir Francis Drake.

A Battle
at Sea

Five small, wooden ships, their sails filled with the warm breezes of the Mediterranean Sea, were making for open water. High atop their masts, most of these ships flew the same flag, its special insignia set against a red cross on a white background. It was the flag of their home port, the Italian city-state of Genoa.

Ahead, just beyond starboard, loomed a massive mountain of stone—the Rock of Gibraltar. The great outcropping stood as a guardian to the entrance of the Mediterranean. Ahead lay the dark waters of the Atlantic Ocean. The ships were headed into its waters, carrying a valuable cargo bound for England and the French regional state of Flanders. The year was 1476.

Onboard the ships, crewmen scanned the surrounding waters for other vessels, enemy ships manned by pirates. Such raiders roamed these waters, looking for easy prey. This convoy of ships might appear to be an easy target. These were not naval vessels, heavily armed for war. These were merchant ships, sailing to distant markets. But those who watched for would-be attackers were prepared to defend themselves. Cannon bristled on each vessel. And those onboard had easy access to harquebuses—musket-like handguns that were heavy, awkward to fire, and wildly inaccurate. But the men on the merchant vessels would not let their cargo be lost without a fight.

The ships were manned by sailors and merchants. At least one person was both. On the deck of a Genoese whaler, the *Bechalla*, stood a young man of 25. He had been to sea before. In fact, he had first sailed when he was 10 years old. He had been born by the sea, raised by the sea, and was now making his living sailing on this ship, this time with a cargo of goods owned by a wealthy Italian merchant. The young man had developed his skills as both a sailor and as a merchant. He was uncertain which would be his life's calling. But one day he would make his reputation, not as a merchant, but as a sailor.

He was Christopher Columbus of Genoa. He had first sailed on similar merchant ships with his father, a Genoese merchant and weaver of wool. Young Christopher had tried his hand at weaving years ago. But he had no desire to make it his life's work. All through his youth, the sea had constantly called him. As he stood on the deck of the whaler, he was excited and scanned the waters ahead. His interest, however, was not so much in Mediterranean pirates. He was about to get his first glimpse of the Atlantic Ocean. He did not know then, but that same great ocean would one day become his second home. In those waters lay his future.

COLOMBVS LYGVR NOVI ORBIS REPTOR

Christopher Columbus had first sailed as a youth on merchant ships with his father, who was a merchant in Genoa, Italy, and a weaver of wool. Columbus, too, tried his hand at weaving, but he decided the sea would be his calling.

The ships sailed through the narrow straits into the choppy waters of the Atlantic, and the Rock of Gibraltar slipped behind them, becoming smaller as the wind pushed the convoy farther out to sea. Continuing their voyage, they approached the southern coast of Portugal, which lay to the north. The ships sailed past the Portuguese port town of Lagos, nestled between the mountains to their north and the seacoast. The experienced crewmen knew that lying ahead was the Cape of St. Vincent, the tip of southwest Portugal. Beyond the point lay the open waters of the great Atlantic Ocean—known to many sailors as the "Sea of Darkness."

Suddenly, a cannon boomed, splitting the morning sea air. In the distance, a large convoy of ships blocked the path of the Genoese vessels. Pirates! The men on the merchant ships focused on the enemy vessels before them and counted 13 bobbing in the water. The menacing ships were commanded by a notorious French pirate, a buccaneer named Guillaume de Casenove. Those on the merchant ships scrambled for their weapons. If Casenove wanted a fight, a fight he would have.

All through the day, the merchant ships and the pirate vessels engaged in a deadly dance in the waters of the Atlantic. There was noise everywhere, as cannons belched fire and iron, while men shouted wildly from ship to ship, firing their harquebuses and crossbows. The air was thick with shot and smoke. Hour after hour, the fight raged as the crews of each ship tried to maneuver into position to allow them to board an enemy vessel and subdue its crew. Sailors and pirates fought one another across open decks, swinging their deadly swords and cutlasses. Blood spilled on the wooden planking.

Then, as several French ships moved in close, the desperate sailors on the merchant vessels launched their secret weapon. Buckets of tar were ignited, and the sailors launched the blazing wooden containers onto the enemy's decks, trying to set their sails and rigging on fire. Flames erupted across the pirate vessels as they continued to draw in close for boarding. The fires spread rapidly, as the pirates failed to contain them. But even as the tar ignited on the decks of several of Casenove's ships, they came in near the merchant ships. The spreading inferno

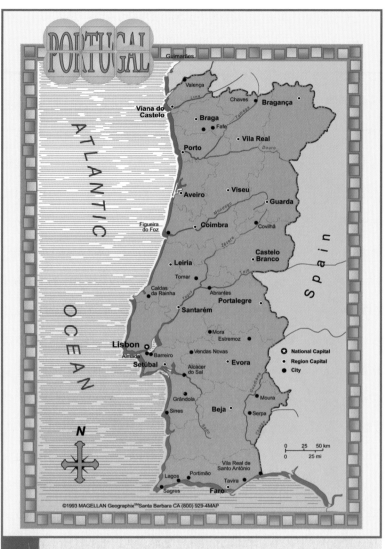

At age 25, Christopher Columbus was serving on a fleet of Genoese merchant ships that became embroiled in a battle with pirates near the Cape of St. Vincent, at the southwest tip of Portugal. Columbus would spend many years living in Portugal.

soon leapt from one ship to another, and the sailors who had delivered the fires to the pirate vessels found their own ships ablaze. Confusion abounded as heavy smoke billowed from the burning ships, both merchant and pirate.

The day was nearly over, and the battle was neither won nor lost. The two battling groups of ships broke off their fight, and sailed away from one another in opposite directions. As night fell, both sides counted their losses. Seven ships had been destroyed—three Genoese and four of Casenove's. The human losses were significant; hundreds were killed. Nearly everyone on the *Bechalla* had died, drowned as the whaling vessel sank into the dark waters of the Atlantic. As the ship caught on fire, the crew had leapt into the water. Those wearing battle armor or chain mail sank like rocks. As for young Christopher Columbus, he had fought bravely. But, as darkness fell, he found himself floating in the ocean he had been so excited to see for the first time that morning. The noise of battle had ended. All Columbus could hear was the gentle lapping of the ocean waves. Dazed, he struggled to keep his head above the water. Something struck him in the darkness—an oar. He grasped it, and held tight. There was nothing to do but swim to safety. But land was six miles away.

Test Your Knowledge

1 What did the ships' flags—a red cross on a white background—signify?

   a. That the ships were from a Christian nation
   b. That the ships were medical vessels
   c. That the ships were from the home port of Genoa, Italy
   d. None of the above

2 Why did merchant ships of the 1400s carry cannons?

   a. To use as trade for supplies
   b. To defend the ships and their cargo against pirates
   c. As ballast to steady the ships in high seas
   d. None of the above

3 What is a *harquebus*?

   a. A type of ship
   b. A navigational instrument
   c. A type of sail
   d. A type of gun

4 What "secret weapon" did the Genoese merchant ships use to fight the French pirates?

   a. Archers in the crow's-nest
   b. Buckets of burning tar
   c. A special type of cannon
   d. None of the above

5 What happened to the young Columbus in
the battle against the pirates?

a. His ship was sunk by the pirates, and
he clung to an oar to stay afloat.

b. He was captured by the pirates and
forced to walk the plank.

c. He took control of the Genoese fleet and
defeated the pirates.

d. He deserted his shipmates and became
a pirate.

ANSWERS: 1. c; 2. b; 3. d; 4. b; 5. a

Birth of a
Great Seaman

Nearly 500 years after his death, his story is one of the first history lessons taught to the youngest of students: "In Fourteen Hundred and Ninety-Two, Columbus Sailed the Ocean Blue." Of all the men and women found on the pages of American history, few are as well known as Christopher Columbus. Schoolchildren learn of his amazing voyage of discovery, when he bumped into a pair of continents he did not even know existed. He, of course, was on his way somewhere else—the Far East—with all its legendary wealth and highly prized spices.

Everyone knows about Columbus. Numerous cities, towns, streets, and other sites are named after him. In the United States today, many cities are named for the famous sailor from Genoa, including the state capitals of Ohio and South Carolina: Columbus and Columbia. America's national capital of Washington is part of a place known as the District of Columbia, named after Columbus. The river that is the boundary between the states of Oregon and Washington is the Columbia, again in honor of Columbus. Other countries have also honored the great navigator and seaman. The South American country of Colombia is named for him, and Colón, a city in the Central American nation of Panama, recognizes the importance of Christopher Columbus. (Colón is the Spanish translation of "Columbus.") Few men in history have been as honored and recognized for their contributions as Christopher Columbus.

But what about the man, Columbus, do we know or remember? There are the stories of how this great Italian sea captain discovered America and of how he convinced disbelieving and ignorant people that the world was not flat, but, indeed, a round globe. But these stories are sometimes a combination of legend and misunderstanding. In fact, when Columbus sailed in that fateful year of 1492, almost no one with any understanding of the world still believed it was flat. Even those with little education knew that the Earth was a ball, that the oceans were connected to one another, and that falling off the Earth's edge by sailing too far into uncharted waters was impossible.

Very important to note

Even to give credit to Columbus for "discovering" the New World isn't exactly correct. The term "New World" was used by those who followed Columbus in later voyages of discovery and arrival. The lands of the Western Hemisphere, which include North, Central, and South America, were not "new" to the Indians who already lived here. Their ancestors had come to the Americas thousands of years earlier. (As for North America directly, Columbus never set foot on any part of the continent.) To credit Columbus with the "discovery" of the Western Hemisphere fails to recognize what Native Americans had accomplished many generations earlier.

Columbus wasn't even the first European to reach the Americas. Nearly 500 years before his voyages during the 1490s, northern Europeans known as the Norsemen (they are often called Vikings) sailed across the North Atlantic beyond Iceland and Greenland and reached the shores of Canada.

So why is Columbus such an important figure in American history? Simply because his first voyage across the Atlantic, in search of a shorter route to Asia, resulted in his reaching lands that were new to an entire generation of Europeans. Those earlier Viking settlements vanished hundreds of years before, along with nearly any firsthand European information about the existence of great lands lying between Europe and Asia.

These Europeans, based on Columbus's "discovery," opened up their New World to exploration, colonization, and settlement, which led to the establishment of many new states and nations, including the United States. Columbus represents the first link in a long chain of events that helped to recreate the Americas into a world region of major cities, important industries, great wealth and world power.

A GENOAN BY BIRTH

Many stories exist about the birth and early life of one of the most famous names in American history. Some are clearly untrue. Others are hard to prove. One is accepted by many. In 1451, a son was born to a weaver and a weaver's daughter, Domenico Colombo and his wife, Susanna di Fontanarossa. The family lived in the port city of Genoa, which is along the northwest coast of Italy. The couple named their newborn Christopher (in Italian, the name was Cristoforo). Even Christopher Columbus himself, more than 50 years later, wrote a letter that states some of these facts: *"In the city of Genoa I have my roots, and there I was born."*[1]

The exact date of his birth is unknown, but it was probably between late August and October. As far as is known, the boy was the first for Domenico and Susanna. If other children had been born to the

This house is believed to be where Christopher Columbus spent his youth in Genoa, Italy. He had two younger brothers, who aided him in his adventures, and a younger sister.

Colombos earlier, they had died while still young. Both of Christopher's parents came from families who were weavers and part of the local wool trade. This was an important business in other Italian cities, like Florence and Venice. But in Genoa, cloth weavers did not usually produce fine cloth. Instead, they made a cheap cloth that was traded near Genoa or in ports in North Africa. Domenico had several

Named for the Saint of Travelers

When Columbus's parents chose the name "Christopher" for their son, they were honoring a man revered by the Roman Catholic Church: Saint Christopher. But who was this ancient figure who became a holy man of faith?

According to Catholic tradition, St. Cristoforo lived in Asia Minor (today it is known as Turkey) and was famous for being very tall. He lived along a river where people often crossed. Since the crossing was dangerous, Cristoforo helped many travelers by carrying them across the river on his great shoulders.

One day, Cristoforo was awakened by the cries of a young child who wanted to cross the river. He placed the child on his shoulders and began to make the crossing. But as the tall man waded through the deep water, the child mysteriously became very heavy and Cristoforo nearly fell under the great weight. When he finally reached the other bank, he told the child he seemed to weavers who worked his looms, including Susanna.

During the following years, Domenico and Susanna had three other children, including two

have "borne the whole world on my back."* Only then did the infant reveal that he was the Christ Child and that Cristoforo had, indeed, carried the weight of the world, since Jesus bore the sins of everyone on Earth. Centuries later, the Roman Catholic Church made Christopher a saint, the patron saint of travelers and explorers.

Perhaps without knowing, Columbus's mother and father could not have given him a better name. By having their son christened after St. Christopher, it meant that the baby who would one day become one of history's most famous sailors was named for a Catholic saint who protected those who travel, including those at sea. As an adult, Christopher Columbus took his name seriously. In fact, he believed his name was a sign that God had chosen him to take Christianity across the seas to those who did not know about Jesus Christ.

* Samuel Eliot Morison, *Christopher Columbus, Mariner.* Boston: Little, Brown and Company, 1955, p. 5.

boys, Bartolomeo and Giacomo (his name was later changed to Diego), and a girl, Bianchinetta. Another brother, Giovanni, died as a child. For several years, Christopher had had no brothers or sisters. When Bartolomeo was born, Christopher was nearly 10 years old. He was 17 when Giacomo was born. All the Colombo children helped their parents in the weaving of the local wool, by working as carders. (Carding wool means combing it, which untangles the fibers, making the raw wool ready for spinning or weaving into thread or cloth.)

Christopher's father and mother made enough money in the wool business to be fairly prosperous, at least for a time. As Christopher grew into a teenager, Domenico may have had problems making enough money. He started several other businesses that never did well. Often, the family lived in a two-story house, occupying the second story, while setting up shop on the first floor. Living and working together, Christopher's family was very close. In later years, when Columbus sailed for Spain and reached the Americas, his two brothers were there at his side.

Little is known about Christopher's youth. He and his brothers and sister were raised to be strong

Catholics. He may have gone to a school run by a group of weavers, including his father, but even that is uncertain. It appears, however, that Christopher did not learn to read or write until years after he had left home as a young man. Although little is known of his appearance, one record describes him as having a long face and dark skin, a long, sharp nose, and red hair.

BORN TO THE SEA

Although his father, Domenico, spent years as a weaver, much of life in Genoa was centered on the sea. Genoa was famous during the fifteenth century as a shipbuilding town and an important Italian port. The port was always crowded with all kinds of ships: trading ships, larger galleons, fighting ships called corsairs, as well as smaller fishing vessels. It was also home to some of the best mapmakers in all of Europe. These mapmakers (the term "cartographer" is used today) and geographers spent much of their time collecting information about new places where sea captains had taken their ships. With each new bit of information, Genoan mapmakers were able to create maps that were a little more accurate than before.

A monument to Columbus sits in Genoa, Italy. During the fifteenth century, Genoa was well known as a shipbuilding town and an important port city. Its mapmakers were also renowned.

Situated in the midst of the great Mediterranean Sea, towns like Genoa engaged in a great deal of trade. Cities like Genoa, Venice, and others were sometimes rivals at sea for trade markets and connections. Even Domenico's woolens business led him to go to sea as a trader. Taking passage aboard many ships, Christopher's father sold his cloth from port to port. By the time Christopher was 14, he joined Domenico on his business trips, which introduced the young Genoan to life on the open sea.

Christopher appears to have taken to the sea very quickly. He loved going on trips with his father and paid close attention to how ships were built, how they moved through the waters of the Mediterranean, how their sails were arranged, and how the seamen used a ship's sails to steer their vessels through even rough seas, high winds and storms.

It is unknown how old Columbus was when he decided that the weaving trade was not for him. The sea was to be his future. As a young man, Columbus was already making sailing trips of great distances. From age 15 to 23, he probably spent much of his time at sea, learning the trade and seeing new and exciting ports and foreign lands. At 19, he served on a Genoese fighting ship in search of vessels loyal to the king of Aragon during a trade war. A few years later, he was part of a crew that sailed to the island of Chios, a trade colony of Genoa, in the eastern Mediterranean. This voyage gave him his first opportunity to see the trade taking place between Italian merchants and those from Asia. During the fifteenth century, Italians were some of the most important middlemen to connect Eastern trade routes to European markets. When Columbus sailed in search of the Orient in 1492, he was looking for a way to bypass these same trade routes that made Asian goods in Europe so expensive.

A PIRATE ATTACK

At age 25, Columbus experienced his greatest adventure as a young man, one that almost cost him his life. His ship, the *Bechalla*, was among several that sunk on August 13, 1576, during a fierce sea battle between the Genoese merchants ships that Columbus served with and a group of French and Portuguese pirate ships.

It was nightfall, and the young Genoan, wounded from the battle, was floating in the water, miles from safety. What happened next almost cost Columbus his life, as described in a biography written by one of Columbus's sons, Ferdinand:

> [Columbus], being an excellent swimmer, and seeing land only a little more than two leagues away [approximately six miles], seized an oar which fate offered him, and on which he could rest at times; and so it pleased God, who was preserving him for greater things, to give him the strength to reach the shore. However, he was so fatigued by his experience that it took him many days to recover.[2]

When Columbus washed up on the shores of Portugal, he was helped by the people who lived in a small town nearby. The young Genoan must have been grateful that he had survived the battle, but realized he was a stranger in a foreign land. What he could not have known on that fateful August day was how his life would soon change direction.

Test Your Knowledge

1 What was the occupation of Columbus's father?
   a. A soldier
   b. A banker
   c. A wealthy nobleman
   d. A weaver

2 What is a *corsair*?
   a. A type of sword
   b. A type of wool
   c. A sailing ship
   d. None of the above

3 What did the young Columbus learn during the sea voyages with his father?
   a. How a ship's sails were arranged
   b. How the crew steered the ship
   c. How sailing ships were built
   d. All of the above

4 What was Columbus seeking in his famous voyage of 1492?
   a. The New World
   b. A place to build a strategic military fort
   c. An all-sea route to the trading ports of Asia
   d. None of the above

5 St. Cristoforo was the patron saint of

a. travelers.

b. lost causes.

c. children.

d. none of the above.

ANSWERS: 1. d; 2. c; 3. d; 4. c; 5. a

A Life Lived
by the Sea

HOME IN LISBON

The wounded, tired, and water-soaked Genoan had very nearly died from the naval battle. Instead, he washed up on the shores of Portugal near Lagos, a small fishing port and market town near the observatory at Sagres. But Sagres was something more. For years, it had been the operating base for Portuguese explorers. The son of King John of Portugal, a prince named Henry, had established a training school for map-makers and sea captains in search of new lands and places for Portuguese trade. Prince Henry died 16 years before a shipwrecked Columbus reached Lagos and nearby Sagres. But some of his school's sailors, who had discovered the Madeira and the Canary Islands, would be seeking a shorter route to the Orient at the same time Columbus accidentally discovered the New World in 1492.

After Columbus recovered from the ordeal of his wounds and his narrow survival, he headed to the port of Lisbon, Portugal's most important city. Its grand harbor, sitting at the mouth of the Tagus River, was one of the best European harbors open-ing up to the Atlantic. Lisbon was, when Columbus arrived there, a busy hive of oceanic activity and trade. Ships from nearly every corner of Europe lay tied up along its wharves.

Columbus did not try to return to Genoa after his sea battle and shipwreck. It appears from some historical documents that his brother, Bartolomeo, was living in Lisbon at the time. He was part of a community of Genoese men and women living there, near the local textile market. The brothers were soon reunited, and Columbus went into business with Bartolomeo, who was working as a cartographer.

What better place in Europe for a pair of mapmakers to live during the late fifteenth century than Lisbon? The city was filled with people interested in sailing to unknown destinations. New ships were being designed for the difficult challenges of ocean travel. Sea captains regularly brought news of their voyages, adding to the treasure trove of information that existed in Lisbon about sea lanes, landfalls, and previously unknown island groups. The city was stuffed with stories, legends, new tales of sea adventures, and scraps of maps, all of which added to the knowledge that seafarers and mapmakers needed to create more and more accurate charts for ocean voyages.

The Columbus brothers soon became known as expert and accurate mapmakers. Often, they were among the first to greet ship captains returning from the western shores of Africa or the various island groups of the East Atlantic. They would invite these

In Lisbon, Columbus and his brother, Bartolomeo, developed reputations as expert mapmakers. They would meet with and gather information from sea captains returning from journeys in the Atlantic and along the coast of Africa.

returning seafarers to dinner or to the local tavern for a drink and pump them for information about their latest discoveries. By collecting all the information they could, the Columbus brothers were able to develop cartography into a thriving business.

While Columbus was becoming an expert map-maker, he was also gaining other skills in Lisbon. He learned to speak Portuguese. He studied the Spanish language, a key to doing business on the Iberian Peninsula (which consists of Portugal and Spain). Whatever education in reading and writing that Columbus might not have had as a boy, he soon taught himself. The twenty-something Genoan did not limit his work to that of the mapmaker's shop. Never wanting to stray too far from the world of sea experiences, he took passage on ships bound for ports he had never visited.

EARLY VOYAGES

For several years, Columbus was able to concentrate on everything about the sea. He learned how to handle a caravel, one of the most popular ocean-going vessels of the day. Its sails were specially rigged for travel on the Atlantic Ocean. Ships delivered him south along the coast of Africa. At that time, no modern-day European had ever reached the southern tip of the great African continent. Some even believed the landmass to be so big that there was no southern end at all. Sailors supported by Prince Henry's navigation school spent decades slowly working their way down the west coast of Africa, searching for its end. All such sailors and captains knew that, if they could finally sail around Africa, they might be able to reach the Spice Islands and riches of the Orient.

Columbus made other voyages, as well. He sailed out into the Atlantic Ocean, away from the mainlands of Europe and Africa. He arrived at lands that had been discovered by Prince Henry's navigators, like the Canary Islands, the Madeira Islands, and the Azores. On such voyages farther out into the Atlantic, he gained experience in sailing through heavy fogs and violent sea storms. He picked up new information on wind and sea currents. His travels took him as far north into the Atlantic as Iceland. In February 1477, he was aboard a ship whose captain wanted to explore even farther north. After sailing several hundred leagues in icy waters, Columbus and those on the ship reached the Arctic Circle.

One of his earliest voyages out of Lisbon may have been one of his most important. During the autumn after he washed up on the Portuguese coast,

(continued on page 36)

Christopher Columbus, What's Your Name?

A merican schoolchildren know the name Christopher Columbus from an early age. They are taught about the man who "discovered" the New World for Europeans. But many do not realize that the great explorer they know as "Christopher Columbus" did not actually answer to that name. Could that many people be wrong about Columbus's name? The answer is: Yes. How could that be? The reason is simple.

When Columbus was born in Italy, his parents, Susanna and Domenico Colombo, naturally named their new son by an Italian name: Cristoforo. They chose to name their baby boy after an important saint of the Roman Catholic Church, St. Cristoforo.

To his fellow Italians, the Genoan who would become one of the best-known seamen ever would be known as Cristoforo Colombo. But a person's name is not always pronounced or written the same when used by people who speak other languages. An Englishman might use the name "William," but Germans write the same name as "Wilhelm" and pronounce it "Vil-helm." The Spanish name "Carlos" is the same as the English name "Charles."

So it is with the Italian or Genoese name "Cristoforo Colombo." As for other languages, they each have their unique form and spelling. In French, Columbus's name becomes Christophe Colomb. In Portuguese, it's written as Christovao Colom. For those who speak English, the name sounds much like its Italian original, but still slightly different—Christopher. As for "Columbus," that name is the same as "Colombo" when spoken in Latin.

Why, then, do many people around the world pronounce "Cristoforo Colombo" as "Christopher Columbus"? One reason is that an early history of Columbus's discovery of the Americas, by Pietro Martire d'Anghiera, was written in Latin.

"Cristoforo Colombo" or "Christopher Columbus"? While most people today use one instead of the other, there are actually other choices, as well. Since Columbus sailed on behalf of the king and queen of Spain, there is another way to say the name of the great mariner. In Spanish, the Admiral of the Ocean Sea is known as Cristóbal Colón.

(continued from page 33)

he joined the crew of a trading vessel that sailed under the Portuguese flag. The ship plied the waters along the "Atlantic Corridor," an ocean trade route that shipped "wool, dried fish and wine between Iceland, Ireland, the Azores and Lisbon."[3] When the ship landed at Galway, on the western coast of Ireland, Columbus may have been an eyewitness to a curious coastal landing. One day, a small boat drifted onto the shore, carrying the bodies of two people. As the dead pair were examined, they appeared to have faces different from the local Irish residents. In fact, they did not look European. Various witnesses decided they had an Oriental look; some said they looked Chinese.

Who, exactly, this unfortunate pair were, remains a mystery. Perhaps, if in fact they looked "Asian," they were Finns, or Laplanders, or even Eskimos. But the discovery helped to set in Columbus's mind an idea that was becoming more and more popular at the time. Among seafarers and those with an interest in extending European trade, a theory was developing. Some were beginning to think of an easier way for western Europeans to reach the Orient, with all its riches and valuable spices.

Perhaps the answer might be to sail west, farther out into the unknown waters of the Atlantic Ocean.

MARRIAGE AND MAPS

The years that followed Columbus's trip to the North Atlantic lands of Ireland and Iceland brought great change to the young Genoan. One of the most important changes was his marriage to a young, prominent woman named Felipa Perestrello e Moniz. Her father was wealthy, a ship's captain and Portuguese official who had studied in Prince Henry's navigation school. Her grandfather had been a knight in service to Prince Henry. Columbus had met her while worshiping at Lisbon's Church of All Saints. They were married in 1479. The newlyweds took their honeymoon in the Madeira Islands, where the bride's father, Bartholomew Perestrello, had served as governor of the island of Porto Santo until his death. The young couple enjoyed their time in the Madeiras so much, they decided to make the islands their home. From there, Columbus could pursue all his ambitions at once. He could spend time as a ship's captain and as a merchant. With his new marriage

The Madeiras are an island chain in the Atlantic Ocean several hundred miles from Portugal. Columbus and his wife, Felipa Perestrello e Moniz, lived there after their wedding. On the Madeiras, Columbus could be a sea captain and a merchant, and dream of his future plans.

into a wealthy, government-connected family of nobility, Columbus's future seemed certain. He could become a wealthy merchant himself. But he wanted to remain in the Madeiras for another reason. The Atlantic islands "provided Columbus with an observation post for his future plans, which were still uncertain and unformed."[4]

The young Genoan was given a new sense of his future's direction soon after his marriage. When Columbus married Felipa, her mother gave him a wonderful wedding present. She handed him all of her late husband's navigation charts, captain's logs, and maps. The documents included valuable information on Atlantic wind and ocean currents. Columbus could have received no greater gift. Such firsthand documents were important. European sailors of the late Middle Ages often had access to few documents on sailing, including maps. Many maps were incomplete and often inaccurate. Stories were handed down from sailor to sailor about the lands they had reached, but often such tales were unreliable. Ancient documents about the high seas and distant lands were typically filled with fanciful descriptions of the people found there. One could read of distant lands where people only had one giant foot, which, when lying on their backs, they could raise in the air and use as shade against the sun. Others told of the existence of "dragons whose skulls were filled with jewels."[5] Good, accurate information was hard to come by.

Columbus, now in the Madeiras, began to dream great dreams about the mysteries of the Atlantic Ocean. He would sit for hours, and even whole days on the balcony of his villa, watching the waters churn along the shore, his eyes scanning the distant horizon to the west. He knew from his new home at Porto Santo that the sun set at least two hours later than back in Genoa. He was fully aware, as most people of his day were, that the world around him was round, not flat. Columbus knew there was no edge of the world where ships could sail off into destruction as some superstitious people in the Middle Ages believed. But Columbus had questions about the world and its size. It was a constant subject of his study.

Test Your Knowledge

1 How did the young Columbus spend his time in Lisbon?

   a. He studied to become a priest.

   b. He joined his brother as a mapmaker.

   c. He returned to his roots as a weaver.

   d. He built sailing ships.

2 What event helped to set Columbus on the idea of reaching the Far East via the Atlantic?

   a. The discovery of Viking ruins in the Arctic Circle

   b. A war between Portugal and Arab traders in the Middle East

   c. The bodies of what seemed to be two Asians, washed ashore in Ireland

   d. None of the above

3 Which of the following best describes Columbus's wife, Felipa Perestrello e Moniz?

   a. She was the daughter of a wealthy Portuguese official.

   b. She was the daughter of a humble Italian weaver.

   c. She was the daughter of a French pirate.

   d. None of the above.

4 Which of the following are examples of the tall tales told by seafarers in the Middle Ages?

   a. Stories of a land where dogs could talk

   b. Stories of dragons whose skulls were filled with jewels

   c. Stories that the world was indeed round, not flat

   d. None of the above

5 Which of the following best represents the Italian spelling of Columbus's name?

   a. Christovao Colom

   b. Christophe Colomb

   c. Cristoforo Colombo

   d. Christopher Columbus

ANSWERS: 1. b; 2. c; 3. a; 4. b; 5. c

Selling
His Dream

COLUMBUS'S WORLD

Columbus's interest in the size of the world, the locations of its lands, and similar questions came at a time when others were also interested in such information. For years, various merchants, shippers, ship captains, and even European rulers had been interested in knowing more about the world and its geography. The time of the late Middle Ages (1300–1500) was one of curiosity and inquiry. This period is also known as the Renaissance. During these centuries, some Europeans made new discoveries in science, medicine, astronomy, geography, and the arts. This new era of curiosity and discovery spurred some, like Prince Henry, to seek new information about distant lands. At the heart of this drive to understand the earth's geography was the desire by Europeans to gain access to the most distant lands then known—Asia, the land of China, India, and Japan.

These far-off, mysterious lands were the only source of such exotic trade goods as silks, various hardwoods, and especially spices. For centuries, spices had reached Europe by the overland trade route called the Silk Road. This camel caravan route stretched for thousands of miles across barren mountains and forbidding deserts. The route was controlled by Arab traders who served as middle-men between the Asians and the Europeans. By the time goods from the Orient reached Europe, they were high-priced. Only the wealthiest Europeans could afford them. There were those, then, in

Europe, including Columbus, who were dreaming of new ways to get to Asia by sea, allowing merchants to bypass Arab traders.

Columbus began putting together all the information and knowledge he had gained over the years regarding sailing, geography, and maps. As a mapmaker, he had seen many maps and knew much about geography. Some of the maps he owned had been copied from Arab sources. As Columbus studied them, he began to develop a theory about the size of the rounded planet and the distance that might lie between the Madeiras or the European mainland and the Far East. But Columbus did not think about the distance from Europe east to Asia. Instead, he became obsessed with the distance *west* to Asia.

DEVELOPING A THEORY

Columbus developed a theory about sailing west, across the Atlantic, to reach the Orient. He used several sources in forming his theory. For one, he relied on maps created by Arabs from older sources. He read several books, including one by a thirteenth-century Italian merchant and explorer

A painting depicts Columbus planning his voyage. Columbus developed a theory that he could reach the lands of Asia by sailing west across the Atlantic Ocean.

named Marco Polo, who had traveled to China and stayed for years in the court of Kublai Khan, the Mongol emperor. Polo's book was one of the best known sources for information about the lands from India to Japan. Another book read by Columbus, *Image of the World*, was written by a French Catholic clergyman, a cardinal named Pierre d'Ailly, who had lived in the fourteenth and early fifteenth centuries. Columbus also corresponded with one of the best-known mapmakers of his day, a fellow Italian scholar named Toscanelli. All these sources convinced Columbus that the distance from western Europe to Asia would require no more than several days' sailing.

But each of these sources had its own faults and inaccuracies. As Columbus read Arab maps, he used a shorter distance for a mile than the Arab mapmakers used, causing him to estimate the distance around the Earth (following the equator, the distance is called the Earth's circumference) at one-fourth less than the actual number of miles. Polo's book was misleading because he estimated China to be much larger than it actually was, causing Columbus to misread the possible distance from Europe to Asia traveling west. Cardinal d'Ailly's book concluded that the distance across the Atlantic Ocean from one continent to another was "of no great width."[6]

As for Toscanelli, he, too, was working with incorrect numbers. Paolo dal Pozzo Toscanelli, known as Paul the Physician, was an educated

This is a copy of *The Travels of Marco Polo* that belonged to Columbus. The book by Polo, who traveled to China in the thirteenth century and spent years in the court of Kublai Khan, was an important source of information about Asia.

physician who lived in Florence, Italy. His pastimes included the study of astronomy and mathematics. He, too, had read Marco Polo. Using Polo's book as his guide, Toscanelli had decided that the distance between Lisbon and Japan (then called Cipangu) could be covered in a ship's voyage of about 3,000 miles. By Toscanelli's estimates, the oceanic distance from Portugal to China was about 5,000 miles.

Toscanelli was so certain of his distance estimates that in 1474 he contacted a friend, who had connections with the king of Portugal, to encourage him to persuade the monarch to finance a voyage across the Atlantic to Japan.

When Columbus became aware of Toscanelli's estimates and theories of a short distance across the Atlantic, he became extremely excited. He wrote to the Italian physician himself, sending off two letters in 1482. Columbus expressed his desire to sail across the Atlantic and prove Toscanelli correct. The doctor wrote back, giving his stamp of approval to Columbus's plan to sail to Asia: "I perceive your noble and grand desire to go to the places where the spices grow."[7] Toscanelli further encouraged Columbus by referring to the Genoan sailor's plans as "honorable . . . and most glorious among all Christians."[8] He also included with his reply a copy of his hand-drawn map, based on a short distance across the Atlantic.

But all these sources used by Columbus were inaccurate. Columbus estimated the distance from the Canary Islands, southwest of Spain, to Japan, at 2,400 miles. Columbus wrote of his conclusion:

"The end of Spain and the beginning of India are not far distant but close, and it is evident that this sea is navigable in a few days with a fair wind."[9] In reality, the distance is about four times that! These experienced, learned men could not have been more wrong.

IN SEARCH OF A SPONSOR

By 1484, Columbus was convinced that he needed to prove his theory correct. He was even convinced that God had chosen him to carry out this great Christian mission of reaching the Orient by sailing west. If a short sea route could be established, Christian missionaries could travel to the Far East by the hundreds. In addition, the Arab middlemen could be cut out of the Silk Road-based trade, which would result in lower prices for Asian trade goods in Europe, including spices. But before Columbus could prove his theory, he needed a sponsor, a monarch who could provide the money and ships for such an experimental voyage. That year, Columbus gained an audience in the court of the Portuguese king, John II. (John was the grandson of the brother of Henry the Navigator.)

John was not only the closest monarch Columbus could approach, he was probably the one most interested in sponsoring an Atlantic expedition to Asia. He was driven by the same spirit of discovery that had motivated Henry the Navigator. For years he had sponsored Portuguese exploration of the western African coast. Seamen were searching for the southernmost tip of Africa, knowing that they could reach the Orient if they could just sail beyond the African continent. (By 1488, one of John II's sea captains, Bartholomew Diaz, did discover the southern end of Africa, which opened up a direct sea route to Asia based on sailing *east*. This, however, would not be accomplished until 1498, by another Portuguese sailor, Vasco da Gama.)

Despite Columbus's high hopes in John II, the Portuguese leader turned down his offer of sponsorship after taking a year to consider it. His advisors told the king that Columbus's theory was "vain, simply founded on imagination."[10] These court experts did not even believe that Japan (Marco Polo's Cipangu) existed. A downcast Columbus later wrote that the "Lord closed King

(continued on page 54)

The New Kingdom of Spain

The Spanish monarchs whom Columbus approached during the 1480s and 1490s to sponsor him in a voyage across the Atlantic were, in fact, the first king and queen of Spain. Princess Isabella was the daughter of John II, king of Castile. In 1469, she married her cousin, King Ferdinand of Aragon, making her Isabella I. (Aragon was in the eastern territory of modern-day Spain.) The Catholic Church blessed the union of the two monarchs, the pope naming them *Los Reyes Catolicos*, the Catholic Monarchs. By 1479, the two monarchs became the joint heirs of Spain.

As strong Catholic rulers, Ferdinand and Isabella could not tolerate people of other religions living on their lands. The same year Columbus would sail across the Atlantic Ocean bound for Asia, the Spanish monarchy completed another royal mission. For several years, these Catholic leaders of Spain had been engaged in a campaign to remove the Moors from their lands. The Moors were the descendants of Arab invaders, Muslims who had entered the Iberian Peninsula back in the eighth century. The Muslims had remained over the centuries, maintaining a kingdom called

Granada, in the southeastern corner of modern-day Spain.

On January 2, 1492, Ferdinand and Isabella witnessed the final surrender of the Moors. On that day, Sultan Muhammad XI left his Moorish state, turning his lands over to the Spanish monarchy. His departure brought an end to over 750 years of Muslim domination in that region. This successful drive to remove the Moors was called the *Reconquista*, which means "the Reconquering." This removal of a Muslim presence in Spain helped to extend the borders of Ferdinand and Isabella's nation.

Ferdinand and Isabella had also been pursuing the removal of another religious-ethnic group from their lands—the Jews. That campaign was completed just as Columbus prepared to sail for Asia. On that very day—August 3—as Columbus's ships sailed from Palos, the last shiploads of Jews were also leaving. The Jews were bound for the only European nation that would accept them, the Netherlands. Perhaps, ironically, Columbus's crew included at least one Jew. He had converted to Christianity, and, as an Arabic speaker, he was to serve as the voyage's interpreter.

(continued from page 51)

John's eyes and ears, for I failed to make him understand what I was saying." [11]

It would be a difficult year for Columbus, for his wife soon died, as well. Disheartened, Columbus had no reason to remain in Portugal. So, he packed up his belongings, and his five-year-old son, Diego, and left for Spain, where he arrived in the spring of 1485, with plans to approach the king and queen with his dream. (In the meantime, his brother, Bartolomeo, who believed in Columbus's distance estimates, traveled to England and France in search of a sponsor for his brother.)

In Spain, Columbus was uncertain how to make contact with the Spanish monarchs, King Ferdinand and Queen Isabella. He knew no one in Spain, except one of his deceased wife's sisters, who was married to a Spaniard. Columbus traveled to the town where she lived, near the port of Palos. When he arrived, he placed Diego in the hands of the Franciscan friars at the local monastery, La Rabida. While talking with the brothers, he met Antonio de Marchena, an educated Franciscan who was well versed in astronomy. Suddenly, doors began to open for Columbus. Brother Antonio introduced the Genoan to the Count of Medina Celi, a Spanish aristocrat named Don Luis de la Cerda, who owned several ships. It was a fortunate meeting.

Columbus asked Don Luis for "three or four well-equipped caravels, and no more."[12] The Spanish shipper was extremely interested. But just before deciding to underwrite Columbus's voyage, he decided he should first ask permission of the king and queen. When Don Luis met with Queen Isabella, she refused to allow him the privilege of supporting Columbus's mission. She was convinced that the Spanish crown should sponsor such an important endeavor. The possibilities seemed exciting and encouraging to Columbus. Little did he know that he would have to wait another six years before receiving official Spanish royal approval for his plans to sail across the dark unknown of the Atlantic Ocean.

Test Your Knowledge

1 What was the "Silk Road"?

a. A European road where silk merchants plied their trade

b. An Arab-controlled trade route between Europe and the Far East

c. A parade of silk banners held in honor of Christopher Columbus

d. None of the above

2 Which of the following books did Columbus use to formulate his theory of a direct all-sea route to Asia?

a. The Bible

b. *Image of the World,* by Pierre d'Ailly

c. A book by the explorer Marco Polo

d. b and c only

3 How accurate was Columbus in estimating the size of the world?

a. He was extremely accurate.

b. He believed the world was larger than it actually is.

c. He believed the world was much smaller than it actually is.

d. He believed the world was flat.

4 How did Portugal's King John II react to Columbus's proposed expedition?

a. He reluctantly agreed to sponsor the expedition.

b. After a year of consideration, he decided not to sponsor Columbus.

c. He immediately backed Columbus and provided all supplies for the trip.

d. None of the above.

5 What request did Columbus make of a Spanish aristocrat?

a. Three or four well-equipped ships and no more

b. Seven ships and all the supplies he would need

c. Five ships and a small military regiment

d. None of the above

ANSWERS: 1. b; 2. d; 3. c; 4. b; 5. a

Setting Sail
at Last

WAITING FOR THE QUEEN

Columbus had to wait nine months before receiving an audience with the queen. One reason was that, at that time, the royal court moved from city to city in central and northern Spain. Each move was designed to save the Crown money, for the king and queen could consume the local resources for a while, then move to another place. Columbus had no money to follow the court around. He set himself up in Seville, where he and Don Luis had first met. When the court moved to nearby Córdoba, Columbus excitedly went there, seeking a direct audience with Queen Isabella.

In Córdoba, Columbus made contact first with a local colony of Genoese. There he met a 20-year-old girl, Beatriz Enriquez. She and Columbus became friends, then companions. Two years later, he fathered his second child, a boy named Ferdinand. Columbus and Beatriz never married, possibly because she was only a peasant girl, a woman "unsuitable for one who intended to be a nobleman and admiral." [13]

After waiting patiently, Columbus finally received an audience with the queen on May 1, 1486. Queen Isabella and Columbus seemed to come to a sort of unspoken understanding after their first meeting. They were not unlike each other. They were about the same age, shared some of the same personality traits, and even had some of the same physical characteristics, including blue eyes,

Columbus appears before Queen Isabella of Spain. Isabella and Columbus seemed to come to an unspoken understanding after their first meeting. Both shared some of the same personality traits.

auburn hair, and skin coloring. But Isabella did not immediately give an answer to Columbus's request. She turned his proposal over to a royal commission to determine whether his plan was worth an investment by the Spanish Crown.

As he waited, Columbus was given a small amount of money each month while the official inquiry group, the Talavera Commission, met and decided. The months dragged into years. In the meantime, Columbus continued to knock on the doors of other European monarchs. He contacted John II once more, but to no avail. Bartolomeo met with the English king, Henry VII, and the French monarch, Charles VIII. Other events took place by 1488 that ensured that these kings would not support Columbus's dream. The Portuguese sea captain, Bartholomew Diaz, returned to Lisbon, having rounded the lower tip of Africa at the Cape of Good Hope. With Africa no longer blocking the way, Europeans could look forward to sailing around this great landmass to reach India and the Far East. That same year, Columbus's retainer from the Spanish Crown came to an end, and he was soon without funds. Nothing was working out for the Genoan seaman and his dream. Another two years passed before he finally received an answer. Even then, he was told no. The royal commissioners did not accept Columbus's theory that the distance was short between Europe and Asia to the west. Spain would not help Columbus.

Columbus was nearly broken by the decision and the delay that had preceded it. He had become a poor man, his hair had turned prematurely white, and, according to one story, "he was forced to burn his father-in-law's charts and maps in order to heat his shabby rooms." [14] Yet, the stubborn Genoan did not surrender his dream. He went to France to see if he could persuade Charles VIII to support him, even though Bartolomeo had failed to do so. By 1491, all doors seemed shut, and he could do nothing but return to Spain to the monastery of La Rabida, where his son still lived. There, as he had years ago, Columbus received new hope. Father Juan Perez, the rector at La Rabida who was one of Isabella's personal confessors, reminded him that the Talavera Commission had only made a recommendation to the Spanish king and queen and that neither Ferdinand nor Isabella had made an official decision. Like a true friend, Perez wrote a letter to the queen, who, rumor said, still supported Columbus and his request for men and ships. The loyal Franciscan received an audience with the queen and spoke passionately on Columbus's behalf. Events began to turn in the weary Genoan's favor.

ANOTHER AUDIENCE

Columbus was finally called to speak with the queen again. Her support was so favorable that she sent a letter bearing her seal and a bag of money for Columbus to use so he could "dress himself decently, buy a horse, and present himself to her Highness." [15] Near Christmas 1491, Columbus appeared before the Spanish court, which was in residence in Santa Fe in the province of Granada, in southeastern Spain. There, the Spanish were engaged in a religious war to remove the last Arab stronghold on the Iberian Peninsula.

His audience with the Spanish Crown went well. Columbus had another ally, as well. The

Spanish treasurer (his title was the king's keeper of the privy purse), Luis de Santangel, had come to believe in Columbus's vision of sailing west to the Orient. He worked to convince the monarchs that, by spending a small amount of money, they could be investing in a much larger enterprise that would pay off handsomely. If Columbus proved right in his theory of sailing west, the riches of the Orient would be laid at the feet of the Spanish Crown. If he failed, the amount of money invested would be small and unimportant.

But, despite such support, the king and queen were put off by Columbus's extravagant demands. Not only did he want ships, money, and men to sail to the west, but he insisted that he be declared nobility; receive 10 percent of all the wealth, lands, and trade that came out of his voyage; and be given the title of Admiral of the Ocean Sea. Suddenly, Columbus and his overstepping stunned a once-sympathetic Crown. He would have no ships. The king and queen would grant no money. After all the years of waiting, Columbus had come so close. But he was soon sent away, still wanting, still penniless, still rejected. He returned to La Rabida,

Shown is the frontispiece of Columbus's *Book of Privileges*, which is a collection of documents through which King Ferdinand and Queen Isabella granted titles, powers, and privileges to Columbus.

gathered his things, picked up his son, Diego, saddled his mule, and prepared to leave Spain for the last time.

According to legend, Columbus had traveled several miles from the monastery when a royal messenger on horseback rushed to his side. He gave instructions to Columbus to return to the court. After his audience with the Spanish king and queen, a debate had continued, led largely by Luis de

Santangel. Santangel had soothed Ferdinand's and Isabella's ruffled feathers, and convinced them that, if Columbus succeeded, his demands would suddenly seem insignificant. When Santangel agreed to pay for much of the cost of outfitting Columbus out of his own pocket, the Spanish leaders were persuaded to give the stubborn Genoan an opportunity to prove himself.

PREPARING FOR THE VOYAGE

By April 1492, after months of negotiating, Columbus signed a contract with the Spanish Crown called the Articles of Capitulation. He was to be given command of three ships, supplies and a crew. He was granted an official Spanish passport. The monarchs prepared official letters of introduction for him in their names. Since they did not know which Asian leaders Columbus might have contact with, that part of the documents was left blank. Columbus was to fill in the names himself. Within weeks, Columbus was given three ships, two provided by the city of Palos, where he had first arrived in Spain seven years earlier. (Palos was actually forced to provide the two ships as payment of a fine owed to the Crown.)

The Fabled Ships

The ships that Columbus used in 1492 were somewhat small for the day, though historians are not certain of their exact size. One of the ships, the *Pinta*, was a caravel, a small, swift ship with square sails for ocean travel. The smallest, the *Niña*, may have been 70 feet long. It had triangular sails. (Most European ships that sailed the Mediterranean Sea were rigged with triangular, or lateen, sails.) The third ship was the largest, a square-rigged *nao*.

The ships all had names, as was the custom of the day. They are, perhaps, the most famous ship names in history: the *Niña*, the *Pinta*, and the *Santa Maria*. Actually, the names *Niña* and *Pinta* were nicknames, as was also common. The real name of the *Niña* (the nickname came from its owners, the Niño family) was the *Santa Clara*. Today, the real name of the *Pinta* is unknown. The *Santa Maria* was actually Columbus's name for his flagship. He did not like its original name, the *Marigalante*, "Mary the Belle," and chose a more religious name.

Columbus had to hire a crew before he could sail. He could not just hire anyone he pleased. The king and queen, in an attempt to save more money on this risky venture, decreed that all men facing criminal charges could sign on to avoid prosecution. In the end, few accused criminals actually signed on. Columbus was fortunate to hire at least two famous local sailors—Martin Alonso and Vicente Yáñez Pinzón. The two men were brothers. Their family owned several ships, and the Pinzón brothers were considered two of the best sailors of Palos. Martin Pinzón was extremely excited about the voyage. He hoped Columbus was right in his plan to sail west to reach the Indies. Although he was jealous that a Genoan and not a fellow Spaniard was leading the expedition, he wanted Columbus to reach the Orient where he could gain riches for himself. According to one eyewitness, "Martin Alonso put much zeal into enlisting and encouraging crewmen, as though the discovery was to be for his and for his children's sakes." [16]

Columbus intended to rely heavily on the Pinzón brothers. Martin was hired to captain the *Pinta* and Vicente, the *Niña*. Columbus would captain the largest ship, the *Santa Maria*. Others were encouraged to sign onto the voyage after the Pinzóns joined. Columbus's three-ship crew would number 90 men in all, including not only sailors, but a doctor, carpenters, a silversmith, envoys from the Spanish Court, and an interpreter who spoke Arabic, which Columbus hoped would be the language of the Asians they would meet. The *Santa Maria* had a crew of 40, while the two other ships' crews numbered about 25 each.

Columbus spent the summer of 1492 gathering his crew, outfitting his ships, and ordering supplies for the long ocean voyage. By August 3, he was ready to set sail. The day was a Friday. He ordered his crew to assemble at dawn at the Church of St. George and take Communion. According to Columbus's own journal: "We set sail at eight o'clock in the morning. The wind is strong and variable. We had gone 45 miles by sunset. After dark I changed course for the Canary Islands." [17] As the three fragile ships sailed west, the men were probably reminded of the name then used commonly to describe the Atlantic Ocean—"the Sea of Darkness."

But for Columbus, it was a day of destiny. Dreams filled his head as he ordered his ships toward the west. He was bound for Asia. He did not know he was also bound, instead, for the pages of history.

Test Your Knowledge

1 How did Spain's Queen Isabella respond to Columbus's request for an expedition across the Atlantic?

a. She supported it immediately and promised Columbus all the ships and supplies he needed.

b. She remained cautiously intrigued by the idea but waited years to finally give Columbus the support he needed.

c. She frowned upon the idea but was persuaded by King Ferdinand to support Columbus.

d. After a long deliberation, she refused to fund Columbus.

2 Who was Luis de Santangel?

a. An explorer who rivaled and disliked Columbus

b. The king of Portugal

c. The Spanish treasurer and an ally of Columbus

d. None of the above

3 What was the real name of the ship known as the *Niña*?

a. The *Santa Rosa*

b. The *Santa Clara*

c. The *Isabella*

d. None of the above

4 Who were the Pinzón brothers?

   a. Two famous local sailors who joined Columbus on his voyage

   b. Two famous shipbuilders who designed the *Santa Maria*

   c. Two Portuguese spies who joined Columbus's crew

   d. None of the above

5 What time of year did Columbus and his expedition finally set sail?

   a. Early August

   b. Late September

   c. In the depths of winter

   d. July 4

ANSWERS: 1. b; 2. c; 3. b; 4. a; 5. a

A Voyage of Discovery

INTO WESTERN WATERS

Columbus's plan to sail across the Atlantic Ocean from the Iberian Peninsula to the Far East had always been a simple one. He would sail his ships south, pushed along by almost constant winds from the north, to the Canary Islands. Once there, he would make a right turn to the west where he would catch the west-ward breezes that blew in from Africa. From there, he would remain straight on course until he reached Cipangu, modern-day Japan. Columbus believed that the Canaries and Japan lay on the same position of latitude—28 degrees north. By sailing directly west, he just needed to maintain a constant course for about 2,400 miles, and land at a Japanese port. At least, this is what Columbus planned.

Good, strong winds delivered Columbus's ships across the 700 miles to the Canaries in about nine days. The only problem the fleet faced was with the *Pinta's* rudder, which came unhinged. Early on, the *Pinta* was proving to be a poor ship for the voyage. It was not in good condition. Columbus searched the islands for an appropriate replacement for it, but he could not find one. He had the rudder problem repaired, instead. The ships remained in the Canaries for four weeks. Columbus also ordered the rigging on the small *Niña* to be changed from the triangular, lateen rigging to *redonda*, or square sails. His crew took on more supplies, including fresh foods like meat, milk, fruit, and eggs, as well as fresh water. They also loaded barrels of dried meat and

The ships of Columbus's fleet were the *Niña*, the *Pinta*, and the *Santa Maria*. Early on, the *Pinta* developed rudder problems, and Columbus and his crew spent four weeks in the Canary Islands to repair the ship.

salted fish. Columbus and Martin Pinzón also purchased goods they could use in trade with the Asians they would encounter—glass beads, brass bells, brightly dyed cloth, ladies' jewelry, and mirrors.

Although Martin Pinzón was an experienced seaman and was capable of cooperation with Columbus, he would soon become a problem. Pinzón was jealous of Columbus. He did not like serving a foreign sea captain. Since the Pinzón brothers piloted two of Columbus's ships, they constantly questioned him, his decisions, and his authority. To complicate matters, many of the crewmen who had signed on for the voyage were friends of the Pinzóns. Several were relatives. Before the voyage across the Atlantic was complete, Columbus would regret having hired Martin Pinzón.

BACK AT SEA

By September 6, Columbus and his crew set sail again, taking up their westward course. They did not pass out of sight of the last island of the Canaries until three days later. As the Canaries faded into the distance, several crewmen "sighed and wept for fear they would not see [them] again for a long time."[18] Columbus and his men were sailing into unknown waters. The great Atlantic lay before them, landless, and the crewmen began to wonder about what lay ahead. Would they encounter "mysterious calms, boiling waters, monsters that lived in the deeps, and other horrible things that nobody could explain"?[19] Columbus was aware of their concerns, mentioning them in his journal entry for that day:

I comforted them with great promises of lands and riches. I decided to count fewer miles than we actually made. I did this so the sailors might not think themselves as far from Spain as they really were. For myself I kept a confidential, accurate, reckoning. Tonight I made ninety miles.[20]

Determining how many miles a sailing ship of Columbus's time might have covered in a day was difficult. There was no way for a captain to know his ship's speed with true accuracy. It was not a true science then. For most captains, like Columbus, the common way of estimating the ship's sailing distance was by a method called "dead reckoning." This required a combination of determining direction, time spent sailing, and the speed of the ship. Direction was generally simple enough. Ships in Columbus's day used crude compasses with magnetized needles pointing north toward Polaris, the North Star. Time could be crudely measured. Columbus probably used an *ampolleta*, an hourglass device that actually measured half-hours. Estimating a ship's speed was another matter. Captains had to guess speed from one point in the water to another

(continued on page 80)

Instruments of Navigation

Today, as ships move about through the seas and oceans, their captains use detailed maps and sophisticated equipment to help them on their way. All the sea lanes are well established, reducing the risks of sea travel to a minimum. But for Columbus, as he left Spain in 1492, he was sailing off into unknown, uncharted waters. He had no maps of the Atlantic Ocean that were anything other than someone else's guess about what lay to the west. Onboard, he had few instruments to help him navigate.

Ship navigation had greatly improved in the century or two before Columbus's 1492 voyage. But what, exactly, did fifteenth-century sailors use to keep themselves on course? Columbus would have had several devices.

The most important was the compass, which had probably been introduced to European sailors a couple of centuries earlier. With its magnetized needle always pointing north, captains could always be certain of their ship's direction. A compass of Columbus's day was not much different than one used today. It had a round face with a magnetized needle. The circular disk was marked off into 32 divisions called *rhumbs*. Each division represented a direction, for example:

north, northeast, northwest, north by northwest, west by northwest and 27 other points. Columbus's compass was on the poop deck of each of his ships, where the officer of the watch could check it when he needed.

Columbus also used a quadrant on his first voyage. The quadrant was a handheld device. It was shaped like a quarter circle, with marks spaced equally apart to represent 90 degrees. Using two holes running along one side of the quadrant, the mariner lined them up while observing the North Star. A plumb line hung from the top of the quadrant. While sighting the North Star, the plumb line indicated the angle of elevation of the star from the ship. This told the skilled sailor his basic location.

The astrolabe was another instrument that may have been available to Columbus on his first sail across the Atlantic. This was an improved type of quadrant, but was more complex. Historians discount its use by Columbus. Many think it was too complicated for him. While such a "sophisticated instrument" may have confused him, he had other advantages. The most important was, of course, his amazing capacity for "dead reckoning."

(continued from page 77)

by "watching an object such as a star or a piece of seaweed."[21] Few sailors were skilled at it. Fortunately, Columbus was one of them. His ability to calculate by "dead reckoning" was extraordinary.

The first week out from the Canaries brought good weather. The trade winds blew steadily from the northeast, pushing the three ships ever west. These were good days for Columbus and his men. In his journal, Columbus wrote: "What a delight was the savor of the mornings!"[22] The days passed without distinction, and the crew settled into a routine. Food was plentiful, and the men ate from a shipboard pantry that included "sardines and anchovies, cheese, chickpeas, lentils, beans, rice, oil, vinegar, garlic, honey, almonds, and raisins."[23] Only one hot meal was served each day, at 11 o'clock in the morning. All in all, the food was average for such a voyage, and the men soon became tired of the same meals. While Columbus and the other captains lived in private cabins, the crew generally slept on deck. Some of the men threw lines over the sides of the ships and fished. Every day, at sunset, the crews on all three ships gathered on their decks for evening prayers.

It was common for crews to complain about shipboard conditions in Columbus's day. His crew, though, became rapidly discontented and, again, fearful. On September 15, the crew witnessed a meteorite fall into the ocean just miles away. Columbus noted in his journal: "Some . . . took this to be a bad omen [sign], but I calmed them by telling them of the numerous times that I have seen such events."[24]

MYSTERIES AT SEA

Soon, the ships reached the Sargasso Sea in the mid-Atlantic. Because the vast ocean currents of the region flow in a massive oval, algae gathers in this part of the Atlantic, giving the water a look that resembles "grass or a vast meadow of seaweed."[25] Some sailors spotted a live crab on a patch of the weeds. Quickly, the men thought the floating green mass indicated land close by. As days passed, no land came in sight. The men began to fear the ships might get stuck in the greenery. Columbus assured them that the green mass was no problem, telling them "grass does not hamper navigation."[26] Passing through the gulfweed took several days.

In his journal, Columbus noted almost daily: "Saw plenty weed."[27]

Other circumstances upset the crew. On September 17, the shipboard compass needles began to move strangely, frightening the men. The needles seemed to be pointing to the west. Columbus was uncertain why the compasses were not functioning properly. But to calm his men, he told them there was nothing wrong with the compasses. Instead, he told them that the North Star was moving slightly, causing the needles to move as well. His explanation appears to have calmed the men, and the ships sailed on.

By September 18, Columbus's ships had sailed nearly 1,200 nautical miles westward in 10 days. With each passing mile, the crew became more frightful of their fate. Land was nowhere in sight. Columbus continued to keep his two records of their progress, underestimating in the log he showed his men. On the 18th, he estimated they had sailed 165 miles. He told his men they had only sailed 144 miles. Some were getting anxious to find land, including Martin Pinzón. Pinzón thought that the grassy sea, as well as the presence of birds sitting on the floating seaweed, indicated land nearby. So he sailed his ship ahead of the others, hoping to be the first to spot land. That day, he thought he spotted land about 45 miles to the north and reported it to Columbus. But Columbus did not believe there was land, so he ordered the ships to keep sailing. Actually, Columbus was right: There was no land to the north.

On September 19, the stiff westward winds died down, and the fleet sailed into rain. Over the next five days, the ships made little progress, sailing under 250 miles. Then, on the 25th, Martin Pinzón again shouted that he had spotted land. Many believed they saw it, too, including Columbus. He dropped to his knees and ordered his men to sing a song of praise, *Gloria in Excelsis Deo*. Everyone was relieved that land was close by. But the following morning, no land appeared. The sailors had probably mistaken a low-lying cloud for land.

These false sightings only made matters worse for Columbus. As each sighting proved incorrect, the sailors became more fearful. Signs of land— grasses, birds, porpoises—were everywhere around them. But no land came into view. Columbus was aware of their fears, their concerns and their general grumbling. In his ship journal, he wrote on September 24: "I am having serious trouble with the crew, despite the signs of land that we have."[28] Many were beginning to question going farther into waters they did not know. Perhaps, some imagined, they had actually passed land, and missed Asia completely. Some began to consider turning back, thinking it insanity or suicidal to continue. Some worked out a plan to kill Columbus by tossing him overboard. They would return to Spain and explain that their Genoan captain had fallen over the side of his ship while taking a position of the North Star. Martin Pinzón was behind some of the complaints and plots against Columbus.

THE MEN SPOT LAND

By the calendar, the men on the *Santa Maria, Pinta,* and *Niña* had not been at sea that long. Since leaving the Canaries on September 9, they had only been at sea for about three weeks. But these were sailors who were accustomed to sailing short distances between ports and landfalls. They were used to sailing throughout the Mediterranean Sea with land no farther than a couple of days' sailing. Three weeks was probably longer than any of them had ever been to sea without seeing land. Mutiny seemed certain.

As September passed into October, the grumbling increased. Writing in his journal on October 1, Columbus noted:

> I sailed west for seventy-five miles but reckoned sixty. . . . The pilot of the *Santa Maria* calculated that we had gone 1,734 miles; I gave him my corrected figure of 1,752. My personal calculation shows we have come 2,121 miles. I did not reveal this to the men because they would become frightened, finding themselves so far from home, or at least thinking they were that far.[29]

A few more days passed. Then on October 6, the Pinzón brothers came aboard the *Santa Maria* and met with Columbus. The brothers told him that most of their crewmen wanted to turn around and return to Spain. Martin claimed he did not personally know whether to continue or turn around. As for Columbus, he would not agree to give up his course. He had dreamed too many years of this voyage, and he was not going to surrender his hope of reaching Asia. They would sail on.

The following day, the morning dawned with yet another false sighting of land. As the day continued, the crewmen watched as great flocks of birds passed overhead, flying west by southwest. It was the fall season, and the birds were part of the annual autumn migration from the eastern parts of modern-day Canada and the United States to the West Indies in the Caribbean. Taking their great numbers as a sign, "Columbus decided that he had better follow the birds rather than his chart."[30] He changed his bearings and followed their path. Although he could not have known at that time with certainty, he was actually setting a course that would take him to the nearest body of land. (He may have been responding to Martin Pinzón, who thought they should follow the birds.)

During the days that followed, the birds continued flying overhead, and the crews appeared calmed, hoping for landfall soon. There had been a prize established for the first man who spotted land.

Ferdinand and Isabella had offered a reward of 10,000 *maravedis* annually, for life. (A *maravedi* was then worth about seven-tenths of a cent in gold.) Such a reward, equal to $700 a year, was a lot of money to Columbus's men. They typically worked for 1,000 *maravedis* a month. To keep them from turning back, Columbus increased the amount of the money.

By October 10, however, the crew was on the edge of out-and-out mutiny. By that date, they had been at sea for 31 days since leaving the Canaries. If their course had been set for Japan, they should have reached it by now. But, once again, Columbus talked his men out of taking over the ships and turning them around. In his journal, he wrote: "I told them that, for better or worse, they had to complete the voyage. I cheered them on, telling them of the honors and rewards they would receive. I told them it was useless to complain. I had started to find the Indies and would continue until I had."[31] By one account of this encounter, even Martin Pinzón gave support to Columbus, shouting "Adelante! Adelante," "Sail on! Sail on!"[32] But his men needed more reassurance. Desperate,

Columbus stated that he would sail for two or three more days. Then, if they had not spotted or reached land, he would order the ships to return to Spain. To seal the deal, Columbus made an extraordinary offer: "If we do not find land you are permitted to cut off my head; that way you can sail home in peace."[33]

With a greater reward now being offered, every man took a place on the deck of his ship and scanned the horizon looking for a hint of land. Those aboard the *Pinta* had the advantage, as their ship was sailing ahead of the others. The grumblings and challenges directed at Columbus disappeared. But the Genoan mariner knew he only had a few days left to reach land. October 11 proved to be an exciting day for the men on the *Niña, Pinta,* and *Santa Maria.* From the *Niña,* shouts came up as sailors spotted a green branch with a flower on it floating in the water. Then, crewmen on the *Pinta* saw floating reeds, a piece of planking, and a pole with carvings on it. Reeds also floated by the *Santa Maria.* Excitement was everywhere. The men watched the water and the horizon closely.

Columbus and his crew rejoice after sighting land. Just before the fleet made landfall, the crew had been close to mutiny. Their many days at sea had made them fearful, and many wanted to return to Spain.

Night fell on the 11th. Then, the most exciting of discoveries. From Columbus's journal:

About ten o'clock at night I saw a light to the west. It looked like a wax candle bobbing up and down. It had the same appearance as a light or torch belonging to fishermen or travelers who raised and lowered it. I am the first to admit I was so eager to find land that I did not trust my own senses so I called Gutierrez [a representative of the Spanish Crown] and asked him to watch for the light. After a few moments, he too saw it. I then summoned Rodrigo Sanchez [the Crown's onboard treasurer]. He saw nothing, nor did any other member of the crew. It was such an uncertain thing I did not feel it was adequate proof of land. Then, at two hours after midnight, the *Pinta* fired a cannon, my signal for the sighting of land.[34]

This time, the sighting was real. The men shouted and wept. Hymns rose up among them. For Columbus, it was one of the happiest moments of his life. That day, in the dark of an October morning, his dream seemed to have come true.

Test Your Knowledge

1 How did Columbus handle the mechanical problems experienced by the *Pinta*?
   a. He traded it for a new ship at the Canary Islands.
   b. He repaired its rudder and sailed on as best he could.
   c. He scuttled the *Pinta* and split its crew between the other two ships.
   d. None of the above.

2 What is "dead reckoning"?
   a. A method for calculating nautical speed and distance traveled
   b. A method for calculating wind direction
   c. A method of map-reading
   d. None of the above

3 What phenomenon causes the algae-filled Sargasso Sea?
   a. A nearby land mass
   b. A slight shift in the magnetic poles of the Earth
   c. The fact that Atlantic currents flow in an oval shape
   d. None of the above

4 Why did Columbus underreport the distance traveled to his men?

a. He didn't want them to become frightened at being so far from home.

b. He was concerned that they might mutiny.

c. He wanted to make better progress than he claimed.

d. All of the above.

5 What did Columbus do to prevent a mutiny?

a. He increased the prize promised to the first sailor to spot land.

b. He promised the men honors and rewards for their service.

c. He told the men they could cut off his head if they did not find land.

d. All of the above.

ANSWERS: 1. b; 2. a; 3. c; 4. a; 5. d

Exploring a New World

LANDFALL AT LAST

The sailor who had first spotted land, Rodrigo de Triana, was aboard the *Pinta*. He, of course, expected to collect the reward for his keen eyesight. But Columbus later denied him the reward, giving it to himself instead. He decided that he had spotted land first, since he had seen the strange lights first. The *maravedis* would go to him. What exactly was the light Columbus had seen shine across the dark waters? No one really knows. It may have been torches carried by Indians while they were out fishing. They may have been waving torches along the beach to ward off sand fleas. Or the light may not have existed at all.

For weeks, the men serving under Columbus's command had fought their fears, complained endlessly, and even plotted against him. But with the discovery of land in the morning hours of October 12, 1492, they were happy at last. The sighting had proven real, and later that day, they made landfall on a small island in what is now the Bahamas, off the southeast coast of Florida.

After weeks at sea, Columbus did not waste time. He took a landing party ashore and laid claim to the island (which he later discovered measured less than 80 square miles) in the name of the rulers of Spain, his sponsors. As sailors rowed the landing boats on the island's sandy beach, they jumped ashore, fell to their knees, and kissed the ground. Then, they prayed. As for Columbus, he ordered the royal

A sixteenth-century woodblock print shows Columbus on his ship near the islands of San Salvador and Concepcion. Columbus called the first island that he reached San Salvador, or Holy Savior.

banners unfurled, as symbols of Spanish authority and power. He called the island *San Salvador*, Holy Savior. Even as Columbus and his men carried out their official ceremony in honor of Ferdinand and Isabella, local natives watched from the cover of the nearby jungle. Columbus and his men had spotted them from their ships at dawn before making their landing. According to his journal, the natives on the island, curious, showed themselves:

> No sooner had we finished taking possession of the island than people came to the beach. The people call this island Guanahani. Their speech is very fluent, although I do not understand any of it. They are a friendly people who bear no arms except for small spears. . . . I showed one my sword, and through ignorance he grabbed it by the blade and cut himself. . . . I want the natives to develop a friendly attitude toward us because I know they are a people who can be converted to our Holy Faith more by love than by force.[35]

Columbus gave the natives some red hats and glass beads. They appeared extremely pleased with what they were given. To Columbus, they seemed quite poor. But they exchanged the trinkets the Spaniards offered for parrots, lengths of cloth, and other items. When he noticed a few of the men wearing small gold rings in their noses, he asked where the gold came from. The natives pointed to the south.

By making landfall, Columbus was convinced that his long-held belief in sailing west to reach the Orient had proven true. He was certain he had landed on an outer chain of islands off the coast of Japan or maybe China. He had no doubts that he had, indeed, reached the East Indian Islands. For this reason, he named the natives he encountered "Indios," or Indians. But he was mistaken. He was still thousands of miles from the East Indies and the riches of the Orient that he and his sponsors were seeking. It was a mistake he never admitted.

EXPLORING NEW LANDS

The island Columbus landed on had no significant amounts of gold or other wealth. He decided to sail to other nearby islands and continue his search, not only for greater wealth, but for the court of the ruler of Cathay (what is now China). On October 13, he

(continued on page 100)

Where Did Columbus Land First in the New World?

When Columbus and his men reached the Caribbean island known locally as Guanahani, they were making history. The first day land was sighted, he went ashore on an island and laid claim to it and all nearby lands for his Spanish sponsors, Ferdinand and Isabella. But a mystery has always surrounded this historic landfall. On which island, exactly, did Columbus make his first landing? It is a question that remains a mystery.

Historians are not certain. Nine places had been designated as possible landing sites for Columbus. Of that number, two are the most likely candidates: Watling Island and Samana Cay. Until more recent years, it was commonly held that the first landfall was made at Samana Cay. The site had been a popular pick as early as 1882. That year, Gustavus V. Fox, a former U.S. assistant secretary of the Navy under President Abraham Lincoln, suggested the island as Columbus's first landfall. In 1974, though, the great maritime historian and Columbus biographer, Samuel Eliot Morison, carried out lengthy studies at sea (he was a former rear

admiral in the U.S. Navy) and decided Watling
was Columbus's first stop in the New World.

But more recent studies point to Samana Cay,
which is about 60 miles southeast of Watling.
(In 1926, Watling was renamed San Salvador,
when historians believed it was the likely landing
site of Columbus.) The Samana Cay site received
support after a 1986 study done by the National
Geographic Society, which chose Samana Cay as
the likely landing site.

There are also problems with the Watling site.
According to Columbus's log, "many" islands
could be seen from the site of his first landfall.
In fact, only one island can be seen today from
Watling. Also, in his journal, Columbus wrote of
exploring his landfall island in a small boat. He
found a large harbor lying between a reef and the
island. For his description to match the landscape
at Watling, that rowboat trip would have required
the men to row nearly 30 nautical miles in seven
hours. Such is unlikely. But at Samana Cay, the
distance between reef and island is only two miles,
matching up to Columbus's journal.

(continued from page 97)

and his men set sail. Continuing to use Marco Polo's book as his guide, Columbus decided that Japan (Cipangu) must be to the south. Before leaving his first island, he took several natives with him, to serve as interpreters and guides. There were so many islands ahead that Columbus was uncertain where to land next. He chose the largest, and named it Santa Maria de la Concepcion, for the Virgin Mary; today it is known as Crooked Island. Natives there sent him to the west, to modern-day Long Island, situated on the eastern edge of the Great Bahama Bank, telling him gold was there. Columbus named the long, narrow island Fernandina, after the Spanish king. But each landfall brought the Spaniards no closer to discovering great treasure.

Even as Columbus and his men searched the islands for wealth, they could not help but notice the scenery. In his journal, Columbus noted how:

All of the trees are as different from ours as day is from night, and so are the fruits, the herbage, the rocks, everything. The fish are so unlike ours that it is amazing; some blue, yellow, red, multi-colored, colored in a thousand ways; the colors so bright that anyone would marvel and take great delight at seeing them. Also, there are whales. I have seen no land animals except parrots and lizards. . . . I never tire from looking at such luxurious vegetation. I believe there are many plants and trees here that would be worth a lot in Spain for use as dyes, spices, and medicines. . . . You smell the flowers as you approach this coast; it is the most fragrant thing on earth.[36]

With each landing, Columbus and his men found more natives similar to those he met at his first landfall. They spoke the same languages, were naked and friendly, and did not have much gold or any other wealth. On Fernandina, he and his men saw natives sleeping in swinging supports the locals called *hamacas*. The sailors thought the sleeping support was a good idea and later created their own hanging beds on their ships. They called them hammocks. With every island stop, the locals told him that abundant gold could be found on the next island.

REACHING CUBA

After a week of exploring from island to island, Columbus decided to split up his ships and send them in different directions. The following morning, a cannon shot rang out from the deck of the *Pinta*, and the other ships soon joined it at an island Columbus named after the queen: Isabella, today known as Fortune Island. Here, the islanders pointed to other distant islands they called Colba and Bohio. Columbus became excited immediately, believing Colba to be the island of Cipangu. (Colba was actually the island of Cuba, the largest of the Caribbean island masses, and Bohio was Hispaniola, the island of modern-day Haiti and the Dominican Republic.)

For three days, Columbus's ships sailed under fair breezes to Cuba. It was another island wonder, with the usual natives and beautiful scenery, but Columbus found "no gold or ivory or Japanese people dressed in silk and other finery to greet them."[37] The island of Cuba was so large, Columbus did not believe it to be an island at all, but the Chinese mainland. When locals told him he could find gold in the jungle interior, they called the place

Cubanacán, which in their dialect meant the "center of Cuba." Desperate to hear what he wanted to hear, Columbus thought they were referring to the "Kublai Khan," the Mongol ruler of China whom Marco Polo had written about. But a trek through the jungle revealed only one more native village, not great wealth nor any sign of the Great Khan.

Here, however, Columbus and his men did witness something they had not seen before. He wrote how the locals, known as the Tainos, "were going to their villages, with a firebrand in the hand, and herbs to drink [breathe in] the smoke thereof, as they are accustomed."[38] This was the first time Europeans had ever seen tobacco. The Tainos rolled tobacco leaves into large cigars (these they called *tobacos*). One Spaniard described how the natives would "breathe in the smoke two or three times, then pass the burning herb to a companion."[39] It would not take too many years before tobacco found its way to Europe, and smoking became a common practice.

Again, another island had proven disappointing to Columbus. The riches seemed just beyond his grasp. He continued to explore the shoreline of Cuba (Colba), certain he had reached the Chinese mainland. On November 21, as his ships continued sailing to the east, examining every inlet and bay, Martin Pinzón broke off from the other ships and sailed the *Pinta* out of sight. Pinzón had heard from natives about an island to the north where the Indians gathered "on the beach at night to hammer gold into bars by candlelight."[40] Often a step away from disloyalty to Columbus, Pinzón wanted to find riches for himself. While Columbus was greatly angered by Pinzón's move, he did not follow after him.

The *Santa Maria* and *Niña* sailed on to Bohio. It was the first week of December. Columbus had been warned by the Cuban Indians of their fear of the people of Bohio, claiming they were cannibals. During the following days, Columbus searched for a good harbor. By December 9, he took possession of the island and named it La Espanola, Little Spain. In later years, the Spaniards called their island Hispaniola. For nearly three weeks, Columbus explored the coastline on the north side of Hispaniola. He sent representatives to local Indian villages where they traded glass beads for more small pieces of gold. They met with the island's natives. The Spaniards noted how these islanders were among the most attractive they had seen so far during their weeks in the Caribbean. They were "tall, slender and well-proportioned, both the men and the women."[41] Two young island women caught the eye of the European visitors, who noted that they had "skin so light they might have been from Spain."[42] They also made contact with a chieftain, or cacique, named Guacanagari. The chief wore gold jewelry, but Columbus wondered if he was getting any closer to the riches of the Orient.

A LOSS FOR COLUMBUS

Throughout these weeks of exploring, making contact with natives, and seeking sites for future settlements and good harbors, Columbus found no golden riches. Everything remained strange to him and his men. Nothing seemed to match up with Marco Polo's descriptions of the places he had visited more than two centuries earlier. The scenery, however, continued to inspire. In his journal, Columbus recorded the beauty of the islands:

There are many harbors on the coast of the sea, incomparable to others which I know in Christendom. . . . All are most beautiful, of a thousand shapes, and all accessible and filled with trees of a thousand kinds and tall, and they seem to touch the sky; and I am told that they never lose their foliage, which I can believe, for I saw them as green and beautiful as they are in Spain in May, and some of them were flowering, some with fruit. . . . And there were singing the nightingale and other little birds of a thousand kinds in the month of November. . . . There are palm trees of six or eight kinds, which are a wonder to behold on account of their beautiful variety, and so are the other trees and fruits and herbs; therein are marvelous pine groves . . . and there is honey, and there are many kinds of birds and a great variety of fruits.[43]

More and more Indians were coming out to trade with the Spaniards, curious about the white men, their giant ships, and their strange clothes and language. On December 22, about 1,500 natives visited

Columbus and his men. The Europeans had no fear of being overwhelmed by the natives, who carried no weapons.

But, in the midst of such exotic beauty, trouble set in for Columbus. He had already lost Pinzón and the *Pinta*. Then, on Christmas Eve, disaster struck. The two remaining ships had spent two straight days sailing close to the coastline of Hispaniola. The shore was ragged and risky, littered with rocks. The men had remained at their posts for 48 hours. Everyone was tired. Even Columbus went to his cabin to take a nap around 11 P.M. on December 24. Several on deck had also fallen asleep.

Then, suddenly, a ship's boy on deck screamed, waking Columbus and the others. The *Santa Maria* had struck a coral reef, and several holes were torn in the ship's hull. The men scrambled across the deck, taking orders from Columbus, tossing off excessive weight, and lowering the mainmast. But it was no use. The ship was seriously damaged. Once the ship broke free, the shore undertow drove the crippled vessel to shore, where it struck rocks. Soon, water was pouring in and the *Santa Maria* was sinking. Columbus ordered his men to man their ship launches and row for the *Niña*. As the men crowded on the deck of the smallest of Columbus's three-ship fleet, they watched as the *Santa Maria* sank. It was a sad Christmas Eve, indeed. The following morning, Christmas Day, the crew salvaged as many items as they could from the wreck of the *Santa Maria*.

PREPARING TO RETURN HOME

The loss of the *Santa Maria* required Columbus to make a serious decision. The *Niña* could not accommodate all the men from both ships. If only Pinzón had remained with them and not abandoned his comrades! Columbus decided to leave several men on the island, while he and the others returned to Spain. Many of the men asked to stay and establish a colony, but Columbus finally selected 39 men, leaving a military officer, Diego de Arana, in command of them. The *Santa Maria* was torn apart, and its timbers were used to construct a fort. Her guns were placed in the fort for its protection. A year's supply of bread, grain, and wine were given to the colonists and stored in underground cellars.

Replicas of the *Pinta*, the *Santa Maria*, and the *Niña* sail during a reenactment of Columbus's trip. Along the coast of Hispaniola, the *Santa Maria* struck a coral reef and was badly damaged. Afterward, Columbus returned to Spain with the two remaining ships.

By the last day of 1492, Columbus was ready to take his leave of the islands he and his men had explored for more than 10 weeks. He was becoming disappointed that he had not found exactly what he had hoped: no great wealth, no fabulous cities, no legendary civilizations, no Kublai Khan. As he prepared to depart for Spain, he wrote: "It does not appear reasonable to expose myself to the dangers that might occur in making any more discoveries. All this trouble and inconvenience has arisen because the *Pinta* deserted me."[44] (As for Vicente Pinzón, he remained loyal to Columbus during the entire voyage to and from the New World.) But he still had high hopes for the future: "When I return here from Castile I shall find such riches extracted from this land that the king and queen, within three years' time, will be able to prepare and carry out the reconquest of the Holy Sepulcher [Jesus's burial tomb] in Jerusalem."[45]

Two days later, he sailed the *Niña* away from the newly established Spanish colony of 39 men, called La Navidad. Columbus had barely begun to sail for home, when Martin Pinzón and the *Pinta* appeared. The ship's captain apologized and tried to explain how he had become separated from the other vessels, but Columbus did not believe him. Needing Pinzón, however, Columbus pretended he was not upset. For three months, Columbus and his men had searched the waters of the Caribbean for other islands and other peoples. They had not found everything they were seeking, but Columbus knew that it was there, waiting for his discovery. That discovery would have to wait until his return on another voyage.

With the two ships reunited, they set sail for home. Then, even as Columbus prepared to set out once more for the open seas, a tribe of local Indians began to attack. The tribe was a branch of the Tainos called the Ciguayos. They were armed with bows and arrows, which they had adopted from an enemy tribe, the Caribs. The Ciguayos, their faces blackened with charcoal and decorated with parrot feathers, fired their arrows at Columbus's ships. The Spaniards fired back, their guns hitting a pair of Indians, one in the chest, the other in the buttocks. The encounter did not last long. The Indians broke off and fled. It was the first violent outbreak between Europeans and American Indians.

STORMY SEAS

After a few more days, Columbus set out once more for Spain. He wrote: "I have decided to return with the greatest possible haste and not stop any longer. Although there are many disobedient people among the crew, there are also many good men." [46] Catching a prevailing eastward wind, the ships made good progress. They reached the Sargasso Sea within three weeks. This time, they sailed north of the sea, and few had any fear of the grasses in the water. The winds proved difficult, and the sea was heavy with high waves. It was winter, when the Atlantic is more likely to experience storms.

Then, on February 13, Columbus "experienced great difficulty with the wind, high waves, and a stormy sea." [47] Lightning flashed across the skies. A violent storm soon rose up and pounded the small ships. For three days, the storm hit hard against the *Pinta* and *Niña.* Icy waters washed over the decks, and the men on deck struggled to keep from falling overboard. Columbus later wrote: "If the caravels had not been very good ships, they would surely have been lost." [48] In the dark violence of the storm, the two ships became separated once more. This time, it was not the work of a disloyal Martin Pinzón, but nature's fury.

In the midst of the storm, Columbus feared his ships would sink. He was most concerned that Ferdinand and Isabella would never receive word of his discoveries. Anxiously, he took to his cabin and wrote in his journal:

> The great desire I have to bring this wonderful news to Your Highnesses causes me to fear I will not succeed in doing so. It seems to me that even a gnat can disturb and impede it. . . . For this reason, I have written on a parchment everything I can concerning what I have found, earnestly beseeching whomsoever might find it to carry it to Your Highnesses.[49]

Columbus then sealed the parchment in a waxed cloth, tied it tightly, and placed it in a large wooden barrel. He did not explain to his men what he was doing. They thought he was sending out a special religious act to get them through the storm. Then he ordered the barrel tossed off the side of his ship into the sea.

When the storm finally broke the next day, the *Pinta* was still nowhere in sight. Had she floundered, sending her crew to the bottom of the ocean? Columbus was not certain of their location, but land soon appeared on the horizon. The experienced Genoan navigator guessed the islands were the Azores, and he soon found he was correct. The Azores are an island chain in the North Atlantic, about 900 miles west of Portugal. Since the islands were Portuguese territory, Columbus did not want to drop anchor there, fearing the Portuguese might take advantage of them. But he needed food and water, and his ship needed repairs.

AN UNWELCOME RETURN

When his ship reached one of the islands, his crew immediately went ashore and headed for the nearest church. There, they intended to give thanks for having been rescued from a certain death in the storm. When the local Portuguese governor heard of the Spanish arrivals, he sent soldiers to the church and had the crewmen arrested during their prayers. Only after Columbus showed the governor his official papers from

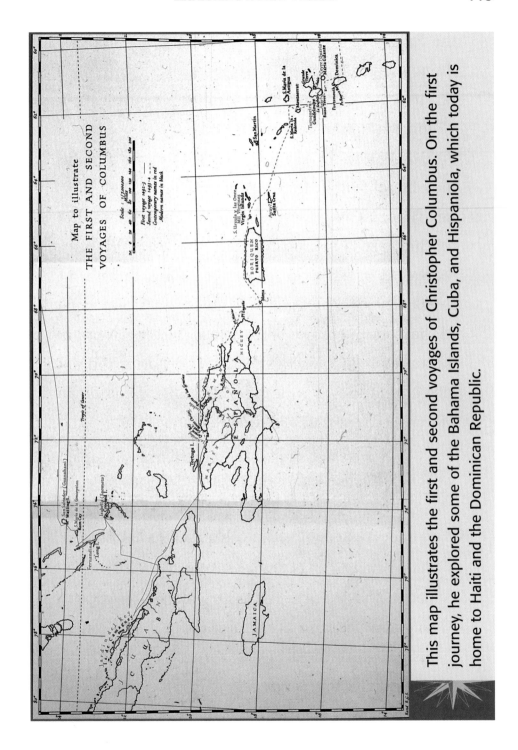

This map illustrates the first and second voyages of Christopher Columbus. On the first journey, he explored some of the Bahama Islands, Cuba, and Hispaniola, which today is home to Haiti and the Dominican Republic.

the Spanish Crown, then threatened to "shoot up the town and carry off hostages if his people were not released,"[50] did the local governor return Columbus's men to him.

During the following week, Columbus and his men bought provisions for the last leg of their journey home. The closest landfall was only 800 miles to the east. Ordinarily, the ships should have reached it in less than a week of sailing. But storms struck again. Less than 250 miles out from Santa Maria, on the Portuguese coast, violent weather began tossing Columbus's ship. The storms did not let up until they reached the Portuguese coast. On March 4, Columbus's journal tells the story:

> When the sun came up I recognized the land which was the Rock of Sintra, near the river at Lisbon. I decided to enter because I could not do anything else. I learned from the seafaring people that there never has been a winter with so many storms; twenty-five ships had been lost. I wrote the King of Portugal [John II], who was twenty-seven miles from here to ask permission to land at Lisbon.[51]

The following day, Lisbon's harbormaster, the famed Bartholomew Diaz, escorted Columbus to the king.

John II had been approached years earlier by Columbus to sponsor a voyage across the Atlantic to the Orient. He could have made life difficult for Columbus by ordering him and his Spanish crew imprisoned for making an unauthorized landing on Portuguese soil. But John told Diaz to give Columbus anything he needed. Columbus was able to sit down with the Portuguese ruler and tell him of his adventures of the previous six months. The court listened, stunned, at Columbus's story. Some thought he was lying and called on John to order the Genoan's capture and execution. But the monarch could only bring himself to express his regret at having not agreed to sponsor Columbus when he had the opportunity. Aloud, he is said to have exclaimed: "Why did I let slip such a wonderful chance?"[52]

Test Your Knowledge

1 Upon arriving in what is now the Bahamas,
what name did Columbus give to the first
island on which he landed?

    a. San Juan

    b. San Salvador

    c. San Bernardino

    d. None of the above

2 Columbus mistook the island of
Cuba for

    a. China.

    b. India.

    c. the Azores.

    d. none of the above.

3 What disaster struck Columbus's expedition
on Christmas Eve in 1492?

    a. Columbus fell ill with malaria.

    b. A hurricane hit the islands.

    c. Natives attacked the ships.

    d. The *Santa Maria* hit a reef
       and sank.

4 What problem faced Columbus and his crew on the return to Spain?

   a. Arrows fired by Ciguayo Indians

   b. An Atlantic storm that threatened to sink his ships

   c. A hostile reception by Portuguese authorities on the Azores

   d. All of the above

5 How did Portugal's King John II regard Columbus's stories of the New World?

   a. He called Columbus a liar and had him arrested.

   b. He hailed Columbus as a hero and held a parade in his honor.

   c. He openly regretted having missed his chance to fund the expedition.

   d. None of the above.

ANSWERS: 1. b; 2. a; 3. d; 4. d; 5. c

Other Voyages, Other Failures

A TRIUMPHANT RETURN

More than seven months after Columbus and his men had sailed out of the Spanish harbor of Palos, Columbus sailed the *Niña* back into that same port, followed by the *Pinta*. The date was March 15, 1493. The previous day, Columbus's ship had sailed past the Portuguese beach where his ship had capsized, nearly drowning him 17 years earlier. As for Pinzón and the *Pinta*, he had reached northern Spain two weeks earlier and had immediately sent word to Ferdinand and Isabella that he wished for an audience at court. He was refused. Columbus had already written them a letter from Portugal, informing the monarchs of his return. The letter spoke with excitement of the discoveries he had made. In the letter, he wrote of having reached the Indies, and he stretched the truth when he told the Spanish rulers of having examined a land rich with "many spices and great mines of gold and other metals."[53]

Regardless of the details of his letter to Ferdinand and Isabella, he had, indeed, accomplished a great feat of seamanship. He had reached distant lands and claimed them in the name of the Spanish Crown. Ferdinand and Isabella wanted to see their hero. Within weeks, he was summoned to Barcelona and their court. When Columbus entered the city in April, he was greeted with great honors and praise. Everyone had heard of his successful voyage as word spread over hundreds of miles. It was the grandest moment of his life:

Columbus's journey to court was a triumphal procession. Peasants and grandees turned out to see the exotic cavalcade [parade] of bold adventurers, Indians in plumed headdresses and fishbone-and-gold ornaments, and brightly colored parrots and other birds. Hired servants followed Columbus and his officers, carrying items of pure gold and amber. In the courtyard of the royal palace in Barcelona, the nobility rose as one when Columbus entered, an honor usually reserved for the land's most important grandees. In the palace's great hall, where Columbus knelt at the feet of Ferdinand and Isabella, the monarchs made him rise and sit at the queen's right hand while he described his adventure.[54]

Columbus received multiple honors. He was given a coat of arms as if he were a nobleman. He was made Admiral of the Ocean Sea, as well as the governor of the lands he had explored. A second voyage was soon being planned.

Ferdinand and Isabella had spent little money on Columbus's first voyage across the Atlantic. Having

After returning from his first voyage, Columbus was received by King Ferdinand and Queen Isabella, who bestowed many honors on him. He was given a coat of arms and named governor of the lands he had explored. And a second expedition was planned.

proven himself successful (everyone, including Columbus, believed he had reached Asia), he was given everything he asked for to mount a second trip. He and the Spanish rulers had agreed on the need to establish a Spanish trading colony on the island of Hispaniola. They also wanted to spread Christianity to the natives. Columbus also intended to explore further for the gold mines he was so certain he had simply missed.

A SECOND VOYAGE

Columbus's second expedition was gigantic. It included 17 ships and 1,200 men. While some of his first crew had included pardoned criminals, this time sailors volunteered by the hundreds. Besides sailors, the ships took in cavalry troops, farmers, Spanish aristocrats, six priests, and an ark full of animals, including horses, sheep, and pigs. Among those who signed on for Columbus's second venture across the Atlantic was Juan Ponce de León, who would later become a famous Spanish explorer and the European discoverer of Florida. Columbus also took along his brother, Diego. Martin Pinzón would not be among this crew. After his return to Spain, he died within a month. Anger, jealousy, and the privations of the journey had sapped his health. No other Pinzóns were included this time. The Spanish convoy set sail from Cádiz on September 25, 1493. Columbus did not follow the same route back to his colony that he had taken the previous year. He chose, instead, to sail farther south across the Atlantic, thinking he might reach the Asian mainland. He sailed on another ship named the *Santa Maria.*

The voyage went smoothly, the weather was perfect, and the ships reached the Caribbean islands by early November. The first landfall was on an island Columbus named Dominica, the Spanish word for "Sunday." This island lay far to the southeast of Hispaniola and the other islands Columbus had explored the previous year. Other islands lay ahead, including the Virgin Islands and Puerto Rico. On one of the Virgin Islands, Saint Croix, Carib Indians again appeared and attacked some of Columbus's men as they approached the island in a landing boat. One of the men was killed. Columbus spent weeks exploring these new islands.

A VANISHED COLONY

By late November, the convoy reached the site of La Navidad, where the colony of 39 men had been left the previous year. Columbus and the others were saddened to discover that the colony no longer existed and that the men were dead. Some of the Spaniards had quarreled among themselves and killed one another. Most had been killed by nearby Indians. But Columbus did not mourn long. He found another site on another island and established a second colony, naming this one Isabella. Little time was wasted returning to the search for gold on the islands. Columbus took three of his fleet's ships and sailed for Cuba, where he explored for two months. But no significant amounts of gold were found. During this exploration, Columbus also reached the island of Jamaica, directly south of Cuba.

Even as Columbus explored, those he left behind to establish a second land colony were beginning to turn against him, just as Martin Pinzón and others had during his first voyage. Columbus had described the natives as friendly and peaceful. When the Spaniards found La

Navidad in ruins and their Spanish brothers dead, they began to question Columbus's leadership. Many had come over expecting to make quick fortunes. There was little gold on the islands. Columbus had exaggerated. In addition, the colony they were establishing was to be a Spanish colony. It would not be proper for an Italian like Columbus to rule over them as governor.

In fact, events were overtaking Columbus. He had reached land on the other side of the Atlantic. Those lands now belonged to Spain. While the Crown was grateful to him and allowed him to return as governor, they began to understand that they did not need him any longer. The next several years would be difficult ones for the great Genoan mariner.

PROBLEMS IN THE COLONY

Even as Columbus continued his explorations from island to island, his colony was gradually falling apart. His dream of discovering the riches of the Orient was fading. Just as his crew had grumbled and complained during his first voyage, his colonists also complained. There were no riches. Mosquitoes tormented them constantly. Hundreds of men fell ill to yellow fever and malaria, which were spread by mosquitoes. Living in the damp jungles rotted their food. Discipline broke down quickly. Columbus, although officially governor, was never present to keep the colonists in line.

Columbus's colony was becoming a mess. Little work was being done, no fields were being planted, and everyone was out searching for gold. Supplies dwindled quickly. Within months of returning to the islands, Columbus dispatched 12 of his ships to return to Spain to bring back more supplies, including food, medicines, and pack animals. He knew, having not found any large amounts of gold yet, that Ferdinand and Isabella would not be pleased.

Relations between Columbus and his men were not the only ones deteriorating. The Spaniards were beginning to exploit the local natives, as well. The Spaniards stole from the Indians, and the Indians stole from the Spaniards. After a small group of natives stole the clothing of three Spaniards who were swimming in a river, a group of soldiers captured the Indians' chief, put him in chains, and cut off the ears of an Indian man. The natives became angry, and violence soon spread. Columbus did not stop his men from mistreating the natives. In fact, by early 1495, Columbus sent back four ships carrying 500 Tainos onboard. They were to be sold as slaves in Europe. He also established a system of slavery that required every male native over the age of 14 to present several ounces of gold to him every three months. Slowly, the native population was forced to work for the Spaniards and surrender their belongings and land. Many began to die of diseases brought by the Europeans, including smallpox. During the next 50 years, hundreds of thousands of Caribbean Indians died.

A NEED FOR EXPLANATION

By 1495, Ferdinand and Isabella summoned Columbus to Spain. They had heard many rumors about the poor condition of their colony. They were not pleased with the native slaves he had sent them. The monarchs wanted the Indians converted to Christianity, not forced into slavery. They wanted him to explain himself. Columbus did not sail for Spain until the spring of 1496, onboard the *Niña.* Many of the colonists were desperate to return to their homes in Spain. The decks of the two ships Columbus sailed east across the Atlantic were crowded with more than 200 Spanish colonists. (The ships were designed to carry no more than 50 men each.) The voyage to Spain went miserably. Food ran out, and some of the men even suggested they eat the natives Columbus was taking back with him. When they reached Cádiz, the locals were stunned by what they saw. The half-starved Spaniards looked like skeletons.

The king and queen were critical of Columbus. He tried to assure them of his further success. He had explored 700 islands, he claimed. But Ferdinand and Isabella were unimpressed. Where was the gold? The spices? The great wealth he had promised them? Even members of the royal court began to mock Columbus, calling him the "Admiral of the Mosquitoes." Columbus's two sons, Diego and Ferdinand, watched as their father was humiliated in the Spanish court. They were serving as royal pages to the king and queen.

Overall, the Spanish rulers were ready to be done with Columbus. They offered to pay him an annual salary if he would simply retire and not return to his colony. But Columbus refused. He believed the lands he had discovered were his. He wanted to return and finish his explorations. The monarchs refused at first. Columbus had to wait until the following year before he was allowed to return to his colony. He did not set sail on his third voyage to the Caribbean until May 1498. By this time, many were beginning to realize that Columbus had not really reached the Orient. Instead, he had discovered lands unknown to Europeans. He had found a whole new world, the Western Hemisphere, which includes North, Central, and South America. But Columbus remained convinced that the court of Kublai Khan lay just beyond his grasp.

A THIRD VOYAGE

As Columbus sailed for a third time to the New World, his health was failing. He drew up his will in Spain before he set sail. But even as events were spiraling out of his control, the aging mariner set a course for new waters. On this voyage, he ordered his ships southwest to the Canaries, then continued southwest to the Cape Verde Islands off the west coast of Africa. From there, he sailed almost due west and reached the coast of northeast South America. Here, he hoped to find more gold. His explorations led him to discover more Indians who had only small quantities of gold. As he explored the beautiful coasts and inlets of modern-day Venezuela, he became convinced he had reached the land of the biblical Garden of Eden.

But it was not a garden of gold, and Columbus sailed on to Santo Domingo, the colony his brother Bartolomeo had built after abandoning the colony Isabella. Columbus's health was failing and, for a time, his eyes became so inflamed that he suffered temporary blindness. After weeks of sailing through difficult seas, Columbus was reunited with his brother. But trouble was brewing again. Spanish colonists were tired of Columbus's mismanagement and were about to rebel. Word was again reaching the Spanish monarchs of his inability to run his colony. In desperation, Columbus wrote to the king and queen. He asked them to send over an observer to decide whether the problems the Spanish were experiencing in the New World were his fault or the fault of others.

By the summer of 1500, a judge was sent: Francisco de Bobadilla, a gentleman and royal officer of the court. When Bobadilla arrived, Columbus and Bartolomeo were away exploring. The royal judge was shocked to find that Diego Columbus had hanged two Spanish colonists and was preparing to hang five more. Diego claimed they were rebels against the Crown. Bobadilla ordered Diego placed in chains and soon took over Columbus's house and his official papers. When Columbus returned, the two men argued about who had authority over the other. Quickly deciding that Columbus was, indeed, guilty of mismanagement, Bobadilla ordered the Genoan mariner and his other brother also in chains. Bobadilla ordered all three to stand trial in Spain.

When Columbus was delivered to Spain, the monarchs were told that charges had been made against him. When they heard he was in chains, they were angered and ordered them removed. They also gave him money to buy new clothing so "he

A royal observer, who went to the colonies to investigate mismanagement by Columbus, sent the explorer back to Spain in chains to face charges. Ferdinand and Isabella were horrified that Columbus had been shackled.

could appear in court in a state befitting a person of his rank."[55] Columbus was not summoned before Ferdinand and Isabella until late in 1500. The king and queen's 19-year-old daughter, who had recently become queen of Portugal, had died and the Spanish court was grief-stricken.

Columbus's appearance before the monarchs who had first decided to sponsor his voyage across the Atlantic more than eight years earlier took place just before Christmas. As he stood before them, he looked like an old man, though he was in his late 40s. His hair was white. He walked with difficulty, as he struggled with rheumatism. The chains, which he had worn for months, had scarred his wrists and ankles. Ferdinand and Isabella listened as Columbus explained himself. Although they were touched by his words, they knew Columbus's future in their New World colony was over.

They made Columbus wait nine months before they decided his case. When they did, Columbus was crushed. Although he would be allowed to keep his titles, he would no longer have any authority in the Spanish colony in the Caribbean, and a new governor was chosen in his place. The aging mariner was ordered never to return to Hispaniola. But all was not decided against Columbus. The personal papers Bobadilla had taken were returned to him. Bobadilla would not remain in power in the Caribbean, but would be called back to Spain. The monarchs offered Columbus money to retire on and a castle to call his own. He would be provided for for the rest of his life.

HIS FINAL YEARS

But Columbus refused simply to fade away, unre-membered. He begged the monarchs to grant him ships to make yet another voyage to the west. He still believed the riches of the Orient were yet to be discovered. Columbus wanted to explore new waters to the south. Tired of him, Ferdinand and Isabella granted him four small ships. The follow-ing spring, in May 1502, Columbus set sail across the Atlantic for the last time. Few wanted to join him, and many in his crew were no more than boys, including his 12-year-old son, Ferdinand. He reached Caribbean waters in just three weeks, his fastest crossing. He explored the rivers and inlets of Central America for a year, but never found any-thing more than what he had already seen in the New World—natives, jungle, bits of gold, trouble, and disappointment. By June 1503, he was forced to beach his worm-eaten ships on the coast of Jamaica (he had already violated Ferdinand and Isabella's order never to return to Hispaniola), where he and his crew remained stranded for more than a year. The aging mariner and discoverer of the Americas finally made his way home to Spain on November 7, 1504.

For Columbus, his days of fame and glory were over. Before year's end, Isabella died, and Ferdinand refused to have anything to do with him. Columbus had money, for he was given a share of the profits from the Spanish colonies that were spreading throughout the Caribbean and beyond. He was not alone, for his two brothers and two sons remained with him, along with a few old friends. He died, struggling with a sense of failure, as well as crippling arthritis, on May 20, 1506, in a rented house in Valladolid, Spain. He was 54. No one from the Spanish Court even attended his funeral. He was buried in Seville. But even after his death, Columbus took one more voyage across the dark waters of the Atlantic to the colony he helped establish. In 1542, to give his memory special honor, his body was taken by ship back to Hispaniola and interred in a new church, the Cathedral of Santo Domingo.

Columbus had spent years trying to convince disbelievers of his dream of sailing west to reach the

(continued on page 140)

The Final Voyage

Columbus's fourth voyage proved as exciting as any of the others he took during his decade on the high seas. He and his crew of 140 set sail from Cádiz on May 11, 1502, and the journey went more smoothly than any of his previous three to America. He reached the island of Martinique, just south of Dominica. Although he had been ordered never to return to the colony at Hispaniola, he defied Ferdinand and Isabella, sailing straight for the colony he helped establish.

As he approached Hispaniola, a great hurricane was beginning to brew. Alarmed, Columbus asked the local governor, Nicolas de Ovando, to give his ships shelter. He also warned Ovando to delay the dispatch of 26 ships that were returning to Spain. The governor refused to listen, not believing Columbus's prediction of an approaching storm. When the storm struck hard, 25 of the vessels sank, including one carrying Columbus's enemy, Bobadilla. (The only ship to pass safely through the storm was carrying gold back to Spain that had been allotted to Columbus from his days as governor of Hispaniola.)

Columbus's ship also weathered the severe storm, but Ovando still refused to allow him to dock at Santo Domingo. With little choice, Columbus sailed throughout the Caribbean, searching for a strait or water route to the west, where he was certain the riches of the Orient lay waiting. He explored the coasts of the modern-day nations of Nicaragua, Costa Rica, Honduras, and Panama. But he found no passage to the west.

As the months passed, Columbus began to behave strangely. He seemed at times on the edge of insanity. But he continued his search. In time, his ships began to rot, eaten up with shipworms. He abandoned one ship, another sank, and the two remaining ships barely made a landing at Jamaica before becoming completely unseaworthy. It was mid-summer of 1503. For the next year, Columbus and 115 crewmen remained on Jamaica, awaiting rescue. When local Indians refused to help them, Columbus used his almanac to predict a lunar eclipse, which he convinced the Indians was a sign of his power. He and his men never lacked for food again. Only after two of his men boarded an Indian canoe and sailed over 100 miles to Santo Domingo was a rescue ship sent to relieve Columbus and his men. Within another five months, Columbus returned to Spain.

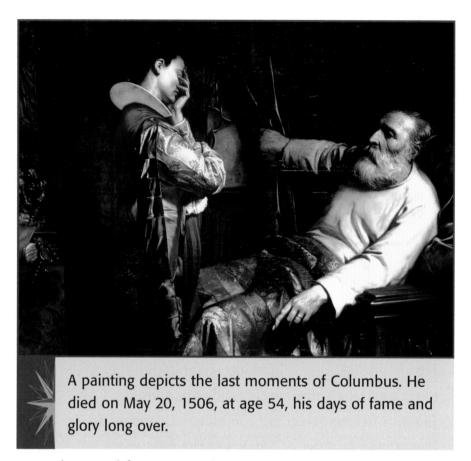

A painting depicts the last moments of Columbus. He died on May 20, 1506, at age 54, his days of fame and glory long over.

(continued from page 137)

Orient. His dream caused him never to give up, as he searched across Europe for a sponsor for his trans-Atlantic voyage. The year 1492 became the highlight of his fascinating and adventurous life. But he had not reached the Far East. For the next 10 years, his search throughout the Caribbean continued. He would sail endlessly to hundreds of islands and beyond on four voyages, constantly finding new peoples and new cultures. But he never reached the lands of Kublai Khan or any other Asian ruler. Their riches lay far to the west, beyond the horizon. Yet in his failure, Columbus was destined to become one of the discoverers of another world, a New World to Europeans, one that would grow, develop, and prosper. That New World—the Americas—changed the history not only of Europe, but of people on every continent. His legacy continues on today, his memory is kept alive, and his exploits remain vivid on the pages of history even 500 years later.

Test Your Knowledge

1 In what way did Columbus exaggerate the findings of his journey to the Spanish king and queen?

a. He claimed to have reached China.

b. He claimed to have reached a land of spices and precious metals.

c. He claimed pirates had sunk the *Santa Maria*.

d. All of the above.

2 What became of the "colony" of 39 Spaniards left at La Navidad?

a. All 39 were dead by the time Columbus returned.

b. The colonists were alive and well and greeted Columbus.

c. Only a handful of colonists had survived.

d. The colonists had built a raft and sailed to another nearby island.

3 What problem hindered establishment of a Spanish colony in the Americas?

a. Constant quarrels and fights arose between the Spaniards and the Indians.

b. The Spaniards were too busy searching for gold to plant and tend crops.

c. Malaria and other diseases plagued the Spaniards.

d. All of the above.

4 Who was Francisco de Bobadilla?
   a. A monk who accompanied Columbus
      on his second voyage
   b. A judge sent by the Spanish Crown to
      observe the new colony
   c. A bishop who presided over Columbus's
      trial
   d. None of the above

5 Which of the following is true of Columbus's
  fourth voyage to the New World?
   a. His health was failing, and his
      crew became stranded.
   b. He found few riches or gold.
   c. It was the fastest of his Atlantic
      crossings.
   d. All of the above.

ANSWERS: 1. b; 2. a; 3. d; 4. b; 5. d

1451 Christopher Columbus is born in Genoa, Italy, to Domenico and Susanna Colombo.

1476 Columbus engages in a sea battle with pirates, is shipwrecked, and swims to shore off the coast of Portugal. He remains in Portugal, taking up residence in Lisbon.

1479 Columbus and Felipa Perestrello e Moniz are married.

1482 Columbus writes two letters to the noted cartographer Paolo dal Pozzo Toscanelli, who believes the distance across the Atlantic from Portugal to Japan is 3,000 miles. Columbus becomes convinced of Toscanelli's theory.

1451 Christopher Columbus is born in Genoa, Italy.

1491 After many years considering it, the Spanish Crown turns down Columbus's request for a voyage across the Atlantic. Columbus prepares to leave Spain, only to be recalled at the last moment and told he could have his ships.

1451

1484 Columbus gains an audience with King John II of Portugal to persuade him to sponsor a voyage across the Atlantic to Asia. King John turns him down a year later.

October 12, 1492 At 2 A.M., land is spotted. Columbus has reached land by sailing west across the Atlantic Ocean.

August 3, 1492 Columbus, his crew, and his ships begin their journey.

1484 Columbus gains an audience with King John II of Portugal to persuade him to sponsor a voyage across the Atlantic to Asia.

1485 John II decides not to sponsor Columbus, who decides to approach the king and queen of Spain.

1486 Columbus finally gains an audience with Queen Isabella of Spain. She refuses to make an immediate decision, turning his request over to her advisors.

1491 Near Christmas, the Spanish Crown finally turns down Columbus's request for a voyage across the

1498 In May, Columbus sets sail on his third voyage to the Spanish colonies. In his explorations, he reaches the South American coast. But his colony is not prospering and, in fact, is falling apart.

1504 Columbus returns to Spain and never sees America again.

1506

September 25, 1493 Columbus sets sail on his second voyage to the New World with a convoy of 17 ships and 1,200 men.

1502 Despite his failures in the New World, Columbus is given ships for a fourth voyage to the Americas.

1506 Columbus dies, nearly forgotten, in a rented house in Valladolid, Spain.

Atlantic. Disappointed, Columbus prepares to leave Spain, only to be recalled at the last moment and told he could have his ships and sail across the Atlantic.

1492   **April**   Columbus signs a contract with the Spanish Crown, the Articles of Capitulation.

May   Spanish monarchs provide Columbus with three ships—the *Niña*, the *Pinta*, and the *Santa Maria*.

August 3   Columbus, his crew, and his ships begin their journey.

October 6   Many of Columbus's crewmen are threatening mutiny, wanting to turn back, with no land in sight. Columbus insists they all sail on.

October 12   At 2 A.M., land is spotted. Columbus has reached land by sailing west across the Atlantic Ocean.

October–December   Columbus and his crew sail throughout the outer islands of the Caribbean.

December 24   On Christmas Eve, the *Santa Maria* runs aground and is destroyed.

December 31   Columbus is ready to leave the Caribbean. He establishes a colony on the island of Hispaniola before sailing back to Spain.

1493   **January 2**   Columbus and his men begin to sail back to Spain.

March 15   Columbus reaches the Spanish port of Palos to return in triumph after his voyage to America.

April The king and queen of Spain give audience to Columbus, who tells them of his discoveries and the lands he claimed in their names. The monarchs agree to sponsor Columbus for a second voyage.

September 25 Columbus sets sail for the New World with a convoy of 17 ships and 1,200 men.

November The flotilla reaches La Navidad, only to discover the colony destroyed and all the colonists dead or missing.

1493–95 Columbus, now the governor of the Spanish colony in the New World, spends two years exploring the Caribbean. During this time, he mismanages his colony, allowing the local Indians to become enslaved. Hearing stories of Columbus's failures, Ferdinand and Isabella summon him back to Spain.

1498 **May** Columbus sets sail on his third voyage to the Spanish colonies. In his explorations, he reaches the South American coast. But his colony is not prospering and, in fact, is falling apart.

1500 Columbus is replaced as governor of Hispaniola by Francisco de Bobadilla for his failure to control and properly administer his New World colony. He is returned to Spain to explain himself.

1502 Despite his failures in the New World, Columbus is given ships for a fourth voyage to the Americas.

1503 Columbus becomes shipwrecked on the island of Jamaica for a year.

1504 The great mariner returns to Spain and never sees America again.

1506   Columbus dies, nearly forgotten, in a rented house in Valladolid, Spain.

1542   Columbus's body, as a special honor, is returned to Hispaniola and interred in a new church, the Cathedral of Santo Domingo.

Chapter 2
Birth of a Great Seaman

1. William Scheller and Zvi Dor-Ner, *Columbus and the Age of Discovery* (New York: William Morrow and Company Inc., 1991), 46.

2. William D. Phillips Jr. and Carla Rahn Phillips, *The Worlds of Christopher Columbus* (New York: Cambridge University Press, 1992), 95.

Chapter 3
A Life Lived by the Sea

3. Samuel Eliot Morison, *Christopher Columbus, Mariner* (Boston: Little, Brown and Company, 1955), 12.

4. Gianni Granzotto, *Christopher Columbus: The Dream and the Obsession, A Biography* (Garden City, NY: Doubleday & Company Inc., 1985), 43.

5. Guido Waldman, *The Voyages of Christopher Columbus* (New York: Golden Press, 1964), 17.

Chapter 4
Selling His Dream

6. Morison, *Christopher Columbus, Mariner*, 19.

7. Nancy Smiler Levinson, *Christopher Columbus: Voyager to the Unknown* (New York: Lodestar Books, 1990), 10.

8. Ibid.

9. Ibid., 9.

10. Samuel Eliot Morison, *The European Discovery of America: The Southern Voyages, 1492–1616* (New York: Oxford University Press, 1974), 31.

11. Levinson, *Christopher Columbus: Voyager to the Unknown*, 15.

12. Morison, *Christopher Columbus, Mariner*, 21.

Chapter 5
Setting Sail at Last

13. Ibid., 23.

14. Stephen C. Dodge, *Christopher Columbus and the First Voyages to the New World* (New York: Chelsea House Publishers, 1991), 60.

15. Ibid.

16. Ibid., 65.

17. Peter and Connie Roop, *I, Columbus: My Journal, 1492–3* (New York: Walker and Company, 1990), 19.

Chapter 6
A Voyage of Discovery

18. Ibid., 22.

19. Susan Heimann, *Christopher Columbus, A Visual Biography* (New York: Franklin Watts Inc., 1973), 23.

20. Roop, *I, Columbus: My Journal, 1492–3*, 22.

21. Levinson, *Christopher Columbus: Voyager to the Unknown*, 32.

22. Morison, *Christopher Columbus, Mariner*, 44.

23. Levinson, *Christopher Columbus: Voyager to the Unknown*, 33.

24. Roop, *I, Columbus: My Journal, 1492–3,* 22.

25. Dodge, *Christopher Columbus and the First Voyages to the New World,* 71.

26. Ibid.

27. Morison, *Christopher Columbus, Mariner,* 45.

28. Roop, *I, Columbus: My Journal, 1492–3,* 26.

29. Ibid., 28.

30. Morison, *Christopher Columbus, Mariner,* 46.

31. Roop, *I, Columbus: My Journal, 1492–3,* 29.

32. Morison, *Christopher Columbus, Mariner,* 47.

33. Dodge, *Christopher Columbus and the First Voyages to the New World,* 72.

34. Roop, *I, Columbus: My Journal, 1492–3,* 30.

Chapter 7
Exploring a New World

35. Ibid., 31.

36. Ibid., 33–34.

37. Levinson, *Christopher Columbus: Voyager to the Unknown,* 45.

38. Morison, *Christopher Columbus, Mariner,* 56.

39. Granzotto, *Christopher Columbus: The Dream and the Obsession, A Biography,* 153.

40. Dodge, *Christopher Columbus and the First Voyages to the New World,* 83.

41. Granzotto, *Christopher Columbus: The Dream and the Obsession, A Biography,* 160.

42. Ibid.

43. Dodge, *Christopher Columbus and the First Voyages to the New World,* 85.

44. Roop, *I, Columbus: My Journal, 1492–3,* 45.

45. Dodge, *Christopher Columbus and the First Voyages to the New World,* 87.

46. Roop, *I, Columbus: My Journal, 1492–3,* 47.

47. Ibid., 48.

48. Dodge, *Christopher Columbus and the First Voyages to the New World,* 89.

49. Roop, *I, Columbus: My Journal, 1492–3,* 49.

50. Morison, *Christopher Columbus, Mariner,* 70–71.

51. Roop, *I, Columbus: My Journal, 1492–3,* 52.

52. Dodge, *Christopher Columbus and the First Voyages to the New World,* 90.

Chapter 8
Other Voyages, Other Failures

53. Heimann, *Christopher Columbus, A Visual Biography,* 34.

54. Dodge, *Christopher Columbus and the First Voyages to the New World,* 92.

55. Levinson, *Christopher Columbus: Voyager to the Unknown,* 82.

Bailey, Bernadine. *Christopher Columbus: Sailor and Dreamer.* Boston: Houghton Mifflin Company, 1960.

Dodge, Stephen C. *Christopher Columbus and the First Voyages to the New World.* New York: Chelsea House Publishers, 1991.

Granzotto, Gianni, *Christopher Columbus: The Dream and the Obsession, A Biography.* Garden City, NY: Doubleday & Company Inc., 1985.

Heimann, Susan. *Christopher Columbus, A Visual Biography.* New York: Franklin Watts Inc., 1973.

Levinson, Nancy Smiler. *Christopher Columbus: Voyager to the Unknown.* New York: Lodestar Books, 1990.

Morison, Samuel Eliot, *Christopher Columbus, Mariner.* Boston: Little, Brown and Company, 1955.

———. *The European Discovery of America: The Southern Voyages, 1492–1616.* New York: Oxford University Press, 1974.

Phillips, William D. Jr. and Carla Rahn Phillips. *The Worlds of Christopher Columbus.* New York: Cambridge University Press, 1992.

Roop, Peter and Connie. *I, Columbus: My Journal, 1492–3.* New York: Walker and Company, 1990.

Scheller, William and Zvi Dor-Ner. *Columbus and the Age of Discovery.* New York: William Morrow and Company Inc., 1991.

Waldman, Guido. *The Voyages of Christopher Columbus.* New York: Golden Press, 1964

Books

Aller, Susan Bivin. *Christopher Columbus.* San Diego: Lerner
Publishing Group, 2003.

Doak, Robin S. *Christopher Columbus.* Minneapolis: Compass Point
Books, 2005.

Fritz, Jean and Margot Tomes. *Where Do You Think You're Going,
Christopher Columbus?* New York: Putnam Juvenile, 1997.

Pancella, Peggy. *Christopher Columbus.* Portsmouth, NH: Heinemann
Library, 2003.

Roop, Peter. *Christopher Columbus.* New York: Hyperion Books for
Children, 2001.

Yolen, Jane and David Shannon. *Encounter.* San Diego: Harcourt
Brace & Company, 1996.

Websites

The Columbus Navigation Home Page
http://www1.minn.net/~keithp

Christopher Columbus
http://www.cdli.ca/CITE/excolumbus.htm

Christopher Columbus: Explorer
http://www.enchantedlearning.com/explorers/page/c/columbus.shtml

Christopher Columbus
http://en.wikipedia.org/wiki/Christopher_Columbus

Columbus Day
http://www.kidsdomain.com/holiday/columbusday.html

Christopher Columbus: Man and Myth
http://www.loc.gov/exhibits/1492/columbus.html

page:

Tim McNeese is an associate professor of history at York College in York, Nebraska, where he is in his fourteenth year of college instruction. Professor McNeese earned an associate of arts degree from York College, a bachelor of arts in history and political science from Harding University, and a master of arts in history from Southwest Missouri State University. A prolific author of books for elementary, middle and high school, and college readers, McNeese has published more than 70 books and educational materials over the past 20 years, on everything from early American canals to world revolutions. His writing has earned him a citation in the library reference work, *Something About the Author.* His wife, Beverly, is an assistant professor of English at York College, and they have two children, Noah and Summer. During the summer of 2005, Tim and Bev took their own voyage of discovery by taking college students on a 10-day journey along the Lewis and Clark Trail. Readers are encouraged to contact Professor McNeese at tdmcneese@york.edu.

William H. Goetzmann is the Jack S. Blanton, Sr. Chair in History and American Studies at the University of Texas, Austin. Dr. Goetzmann was awarded the Joseph Pulitzer and Francis Parkman Prizes for American History, 1967, for *Exploration and Empire: The Explorer and the Scientist in the Winning of the American West.* In 1999, he was elected a member of the American Philosophical Society, founded by Benjamin Franklin in 1743, to honor achievement in the sciences and humanities.